D0394688

TEACHER

TEACHER

Two Years in the Mississippi Delta

Michael Copperman

University Press of Mississippi   Jackson

The University Press of Mississippi is a member
of the Association of American University Presses.

First printing 2016

∞

Library of Congress Cataloging-in-Publication Data

Names: Copperman, Michael, author.
Title: Teacher : two years in the Mississippi Delta / Michael Copperman.
Description: Jackson : University Press of Mississippi, 2016.
Identifiers: LCCN 2015043303 (print) | LCCN 2016004196 (ebook) | ISBN
    9781496805850 (cloth : alk. paper) | ISBN 9781496805867 (epub single) |
    ISBN 9781496805874 (epub institutional) | ISBN 9781496805881 (pdf single)
    | ISBN 9781496805898 (pdf institutional)
Subjects: LCSH: Education, Elementary—Mississippi—Delta (Region) |
    Education, Rural—Mississippi—Delta (Region) | Children with social
    disabilities—Education—Mississippi—Delta (Region) | Elementary school
    teaching—Mississippi—Delta (Region) | Elementary school
    teachers—Mississippi—Delta (Region) | Teach for America (Project) |
    Delta (Miss. : Region)—Race relations. | Delta (Miss. : Region)—Social
    conditions. | Copperman, Michael.
Classification: LCC LA314.D45 C67 2016 (print) | LCC LA314.D45 (ebook) | DDC
    371.10209762—dc23
LC record available at http://lccn.loc.gov/2015043303

British Library Cataloging-in-Publication Data available

There are some blows so violent—
I can't answer!

—César Vallejo, "The Black Riders"

CONTENTS

Past, Present, Future

My past a broken bicycle
laying on the side of the road.

My present a firecracker
that shoot light high in the sky.

My future a perfect test
in a pile of tests that the
teacher never gone grade.

—*Fourth-grade public school student, Mississippi*

TEACHER

UNCERTAINTY

I follow the freeway from the Memphis airport, and every car seems a tall-tired, window-tinted Ford with a blond man or woman peering through my windshield, or a fender-bent, paint-chipped sedan full of blacks who meet and meet my gaze as they pass. I slip out the low end of the city, the miles of gas-station-convenience-store-fried-chicken joints, the Family Dollar and Save-a-Lot and Save-U-Mores and clubs with hand-lettered signs advertising "Free Bluse," turn onto the Reverend James L Netters Parkway that becomes Highway 61, and watch buildings lose integrity, roofs, walls, and porches folding, bending, giving way. It's imminent in the roll of the tires to pitted concrete: the Delta, King Cotton, land of the lyncher, black men, the blues. Trees begin along the roadway, first a scattering between structures, then tunnels of dense, overhanging growth—great, straight, kudzued trees, passage without exit.

Suddenly there's open plain and a girdered bank of power lines over the freeway, wires hung with arterial strands of kudzu cut from the root but left aerial. And then the sign: "Mississippi—It's Like Coming Home." The air conditioning is cold, and out the tinted windows of the rental Chevy heat waves shiver the furrowed fields, the stalks brown with October but the bolls swollen, flights of cotton bursting free like torn feather pillows. Clouds of cotton rise behind the car, leave only an erasing white against the blue sky, and ahead only relentless asphalt and dust. I drive like this for hours, keep my eyes fixed ahead for signs I'm near. Finally, through Rosewood and past, and back through the flat fields, here is the catfish plant puffing steam from twin chimneys, and then the sign, "Welcome to Promise," and it all seems the same, even to the dusty Ford doing twenty under the speed limit that I come on and get caught behind, even to the driver's helmet of blond hair, and then, as he cranes his head about to see me, the stare, disbelieving and irate, as if to say, Chinaman, you know you still don't belong.

It's been six years since I drove this long road from Memphis through the fields of cotton, the depthless sky. When I left Promise that June of my twenty-fourth birthday, everything I owned in the back of my car, I didn't feel freed so much as on the lam from responsibility. Now the Delta branch of Teach For America has invited me all this way for an alumni weekend to celebrate a donation and to observe their professional development, and I couldn't turn down the chance to return. I've continued in education, teaching low-income, first-generation, at-risk students of color at the University of Oregon in an effort to retain them, but the origins of that path lead back here. Returning, I've thought of everything I can say about these last years teaching at-risk students of color at the university, how deserving children can make good on opportunity if it's offered. That, and it's an excuse to return, to see if it's all still there: the town and school, the kids. It's absurd, but I have the sense that Promise-Upper couldn't have gone on without me. The meeting is scheduled in Helena, Arkansas, much later in the day, so I've left myself the afternoon to drive to Promise.

I'm nervous about interacting with the new teachers, remember being one that August, freshly graduated from college: wide eyed and callow, full of confidence in the ability to lead every last child to the promised land of educational achievement. In thinking of what to say to them, I've talked my way through blistering condemnations of hubris and naïveté and unrealistic expectations. I imagine I can warn them of the true struggle ahead, of the high stakes and terrible odds, the need above all to endure. I have a good angle: am going to tell of Serenity Warner, who came to my classroom reading at a fourth-grade level and left at an eleventh-grade level, who won the Promise-Upper reading contest by a wide margin. "You will alter a child's horizons," I'll declare. "Change a child's future."

I come to the run of the highway strip, the Double-Quick and Conoco and Waffle House, the Grace Food Store. Black people mill about parked cars, heads down, shielding their eyes and noses from the dust of passing cars. At the next light I turn on Main, a queue of two-story colonials with wraparound porches, the magnolias with trunks like castle turrets, and only one black man now, a white-haired fellow in blue coveralls pushing a mower over the bright green lawn in front of a white house with scalloped blue trim, while a young blonde girl in a yellow sundress watches from the porch.

At Magnolia I turn and stop in front of the house I rented, a blue rancho by the black ninth-grade school. The house is empty, the windows dark: no tenant now. The white Academy football field across the street is still hemmed in by a chain-link fence topped in hoops of razor wire. When the Supreme Court ruled sixteen years after *Brown v. Board* that it applied even in the Delta, Triangle County's white school board sold the field to the newly formed Academy for one dollar. White football players run drills inside the fence, while outside a dozen black kids hang loose-handed on the chain-link fence. They don't yell or jeer, just watch the players race from line to line over the immaculate grass.

I make for downtown. Sidewalks bake in the sun, but nobody walks the lonely false-fronts, the windows boarded, everything abandoned in the gutted center. Then there's the bridge across the bayou, the lowest point, the opaque green surface punctured by cypress knees, the bump of the train tracks and the black side of town—Felicity Street. Old men and women stare from the shade of porches sagging to the dirt yards, the rusting roofs of shotgun shacks. A white-haired man sits in a dirt yard in an easy chair, three or four children in shorts circling about him. Two women stand on an unshaded porch, one with a hairnet gesturing expansively, the other nodding in affirmation. A group of teenage boys swagger along the side of the road, the baggy folds of their pants pooling above impossibly white shoes, their heads wrapped with handkerchiefs or shaved bald so you can see the contours of their skulls. Trailing behind them, three girls of the same age sway jauntily along, legs long and muscular and overexposed, the girl in the middle pushing a baby stroller, the baby hidden from sight. And then, at street's end, the school's familiar sign mounted to the razor-wire fence: "Promise-Upper Elementary," declared in blue and black, a smiling koala ascending a branch that ends abruptly near the top of the sign.

The school spreads in cinder-block chunks bridged by covered walkways. There are no trees or shrubs along the concrete walkways, only browned grass in the spaces between buildings, and at one end of the kickball field, a picnic table and a wooden playground structure where a weathered black tire dangles from three ropes. On the wall by the office a sign declares:

No one was born a loser
No one was born a winner
Everyone was born a chooser

I grimace—do I teach the choosers at the university, those children who kept their heads down and seized success, or are they winners of a lottery that offers few tickets and confers only occasional prizes? How many kids from Promise-Upper have a choice? I look past the sign, see the long, low run of the fourth-grade hall, the window of what was my classroom. It's still there. I close my eyes and see it:

The classroom approaching eight a.m. The rattle of the heater, an inadequate heat. Orange light at the rear windows, throwing stars off the razor-wire fence, diamond shadows to the concrete yard. In the back of the classroom, twenty-six coats on hooks. The bell rings in the tasks at hand, and every student is already at a desk, at work on the morning math. A dozen review problems, a multiplication table, some long division, the daily word problem: Deshawn buys 234 donuts. He fills boxes with a dozen donuts each. How many boxes will he have, and how many leftover donuts will he eat?

The only sound in the room is pencil to paper. Felicia, long finished, lolls in her seat, legs twisted beneath the desk. I glance at her and she grins, reaches beneath her desk for her book, opens to the bookmarked page, and begins to read, performing for my benefit, lips forming the words to stress her effort. Serenity, back in the corner, has her book out too. I hide my smile. Now a hand: Deshawn, big-eyed, enthusiastic about his word problem.

"What a dozen is?"

"Twelve." He nods, begins to write. "One minute left," I call to a collective intake of breath, the mounting scratch of graphite. Solomon's mouth works a hundred words per minute, then his pencil clatters to the desk, and he reaches a hand to his hair, slicks it back with satisfaction.

"Please stand."

A creaking of chairs, and two dozen straight backs, faces turned to the dangling red, white, and blue, and every hand to a heart except Solomon, who's somehow figured his heart on the right side. State law has us pledging to country, under God and indivisible, freedom of life within razor-wire fences and shotgun shacks and flat, open fields. And then the expectant pause as I walk to the front of the room and all of us begin together: "I pledge allegiance to the class, to work together and never rest . . ." This pledge is always louder, a reckless volume; I know they can hear us next door, the sound shivering through cinder block. The call and response is roared: *"What's today?"* "A chance to learn." *"What's tomorrow?"* "Too late!" *"When's the time?"* "Now." *"Whose education?"* "Our education!" *"Whose future?"* "Ours!"

I blink my eyes open, see now only the sun striking diamonds off what was my classroom window. Now, another teacher owns that room; now, my kids are at the high school. I drive Felicity Street again, peering along gravel side streets with empty lots in blank alleys, yellow dust rising behind the car in air lazy with heat, and come on a little girl in a pink jumpsuit, her cornrows bouncing as she dances to music I can't hear in the closed car, arms raised and legs kicking as she pops Memphis two-step and four-step jook, turns and spins, gets low and lower still. Behind her, leaning to the brick wall of the tenement, is a thin, awkward girl with glasses, her hair pulled back into a single unflattering braid. She wears a faded red uniform polo and khakis, her arms crossed across her chest as she watches the girl in the jumpsuit twist and twirl and reach her fingers for the sky, her eyes following the dancer's every move with a disturbing intensity, a longing to be the jumpsuited, cavorting girl, and I think of Serenity Warner and the difference between winners and losers.

Finally, I start the car and drive the streets again. I frequently took children home through these potholed streets and look now for the kids I taught, though they'll be grown now, teenagers, and who knows if I'll recognize them at all.

Children turn to point from the sides of the road, and I do not know them but I look anyway for recognition in their eyes, and find only fascination, innocence, excitement. I search for landmarks and find them readily: Deshawn's house, nobody outside I can see. Mrs. Mason's place, better kept than the rest, the siding new, the lawn almost green.

And then I come to Serenity's house and stop the car, stunned.

The porch and front door and the left side of the front wall are still there, burnt black and umber at the edges. The roof is gone, everything but the frame taken to ashes and rubble. I leap from the car, leave it still running as if there's something to be done, and stand in the still air with the motor chugging behind me and the sun beating down and all the ruin before me, and there's nothing to speak of how or why or what. Nothing to reveal what happened. And suddenly, I'm filled with the story I didn't intend to tell.

Serenity loved reading more than any other student in my class. She wasn't the fastest reader, or the brightest student—that honor was reserved for Felicia Jackson, my evil genius. The difference was that Serenity loved reading, loved books. She was poor—from a family, the Warners, who made the baseline poverty of other children seem First World. Serenity's uniform shirts were spotted with bleach stains and grease stains; often she smelled, a sour, intestinal scent of body, though it was hard to say if that was because she hadn't showered or her clothes hadn't been washed. Her ill-fitting khaki pants bunched at the waist, held there by a fraying woven belt, the cloth flat and baggy and unraveling at the bottom, where it appeared to have been scissored short: a larger hand-me-down cut to length but not to size. One pair of her khakis had holes at the pocket line, and though Serenity went to lengths to hide them, sometimes a view of her cotton underwear was evident. More than once, I'd caught a child snickering or mocking her, and had pulled them into the hall and lectured them on the shame of such cruelty. Serenity handled herself well with the insults: she ignored them. Only Felicia, with her talent for finding vulnerability, could get to Serenity, whom she called "Raggedy S," and "Smellity," and "Serene-nasty." These insults only worked once, when Felicia first deployed them; other children picked them up, but by then Serenity was hardened against them.

Perhaps this harassment was the reason Serenity loved so much to read: in books lay sanctuary from the unpleasant present. She made my classroom by seven-thirty each morning, after dropping off her little brother Willie at his third-grade classroom. She greeted me with a measured smile and a wave, and immediately barricaded herself in beanbags at the corner behind my desk and opened her book. She kept a book at her desk, and our agreement was that she could read the moment she finished her work. She gave me her book to hold at the lines for lunch so that she could read at recess, where she'd either stay near me so that I'd keep the other children from harassing her, or sit with her back at the corner of the fence so as to be able to see the other children coming.

After school, she fetched her brother from the lower school and stayed as long as she could—often until six or seven o'clock in the evening. She kept an eye on Willie, who was a bundle of energy and angst, a pain for me to manage, though I let him stay anyway. She was careful, too, to find a place away from Felicia, who often stayed afternoons helping clean the classroom and prepare for the next day. Serenity had, she said, "nothing to go to"—she was solely responsible for Willie through the evening, and no adult ever checked on her. When asked where her mother was, she'd shrug and say quietly, "Somewhere." I asked around and found that the word among the children was that Serenity's mother was "always messed up," that folks laughed at her behind her back, sometimes mocked her to her face.

I was determined to reach her, to create a safe space for her to learn. She deserved a chance, that much was clear, and every book I put in her hands was enrichment. I'd go to her when she was reading and ask questions about her latest book, and her answers revealed a passion for the fantastic. She liked to be carried away into a world with new rules and possibilities, realms of fantasy and magic and inevitable happy endings. "Them wizard children, they got the spells and smarts to make all that evil go down," she'd say. "They face they trouble and find an answer, always." When I praised these connections, told her what an excellent reader she was, she thanked me, impatient to return to the book, not wanting to talk about what she could experience. And so, mostly, I let her read.

After all, I'd seen the house where she and Willie lived— I often took them home after school, since sometimes children would harass them if they walked. Their place was an eyesore in a neighborhood of aging shacks and tin-roofed hovels. The walls of the house were green with decay, and the windows had been sloppily boarded; the roof was a series of mismatched, overlapped sheets of plastic. The dirt yard was filled with food wrappers and empty beer cans tossed in at the invitation of bags of garbage piled there to head height. The smell of rot was gagging even from the car. Serenity would thank me, swing her book bag on, take Willie by the hand, and stride into that yard past the hill of garbage, while I stood and waited for them to make it safe inside.

One week in my unit on poetry, we wrote past, present, and future poems. I read Serenity's over her shoulder:

My past a pile of trash
baking in the sun.
My present a book
that hurt to read.
My future a slap to the face.

I stood, stunned, then bent over her desk. "Is that really true, honey?"

She put her chin to her chest and said nothing. Finally I saw that she was staring at my silk tie, which had fallen across her hand. "Sorry," I said.

"That—ok." She folded her hands on her desk.

"But—your poem, Serenity."

She turned to stare out the window where the day was blindingly bright. Her voice was small and quiet. "It just some words. Don't you worry, Mr. Copperman. I just like the way it sound."

I put my hand on hers. "Well, Serenity, I like the way it sounds, too."

She met my gaze—something she rarely did. There was a defiant firmness in her eyes, the recognition of something vast and awful that she faced with as much dignity as she could. "If it sound good, then I guess it a good poem."

I walk the ruin of Serenity's house for half an hour. The fire is old, the ashes and soot dusted over and washed out, so that when I touch the burnt support beams they barely mark my hand. I find the metal frame of a bed, the coil of springs half buried in dirt, here a burnt can or picture frame or oven rack, indistinguishable shards of glass that might have been beer bottles or cups or bowls. Nothing of significance. I picture the house as it was, imagine the flames eating it from within. It would have gone up quick—those old, dry boards, already part air. Through the standing frame there are patches of sky, the shiny leaves of the neighbor's magnolia, my rental car still running. Everything is open.

I cast Serenity as a success story: the girl from the poor family who made good on the opportunity of my classroom. In my telling I reached her, lifted her from her small circumstances into a bright, boundless future. I made her an anecdote, and so forgot her.

In this windowless house, Serenity huddled reading of a different world, dreamt herself in a different life. It's pretty to picture her the night of the fire, seizing that dress in her free hand and leading Willie out the door as the heat and smoke mounted: crossing the threshold to safety. There's no sign she died here—just as there is no assurance she wasn't trapped by the rising flames and faced her fate like a heroine, confirmed in the end she always knew was coming.

I ask around. Nobody died in the fire. The family left for a time, and later, somebody's cousin in Orange Mound heard from somebody else that Serenity and Willie were put temporarily in foster care, and that's all anyone is sure of.

Back in the car, I sit in the cab and take comfort in the uncertainty: Serenity's alive, and could be anywhere at all. Then I close my eyes and imagine her that night, standing in the street watching the fire consume everything she's ever known. After a time she turns from the heat, stares into the surrounding dark, and believes, for the first time, in escape.

THE FIRST YEAR

INTO THE DELTA

Educational inequality in the United States is easy to define by numbers: the disparity in spending between the wealthiest and poorest districts is some $9,000 per student per year. By the age of nine, a child from a low-income area is, on average, three grade levels behind his or her peers in middle- and upper-income areas. That same nine-year-old child is already some seven times less likely to graduate from college than a child not born into poverty.

These are shocking statistics, but awareness of numbers doesn't create change. A new crisis regarding the failure of public education, oddly similar in substance to the previous one, is declared every few years, and for a time politicians hem and haw, reporters dust off Jonathan Kozol's *Savage Inequalities* and attest to its relevance, and educators find themselves for a moment the center of discussion, if only in light of their failings. Then the moment passes, the media moves on, and things continue as they were.

Teach For America is an organization dedicated to placing recent college graduates as teachers in underresourced areas for two years. Its mission is to create a movement dedicated to the vision that one day, all children of this nation, regardless of the color of their skin or how much privilege they were born into, will have the opportunity to attain an excellent education. The program is exceptionally selective: typically, the acceptance rate is close to one applicant in twelve, a more competitive entry rate than most Ivy League schools can boast. In 2002, I applied and interviewed and was deemed an appropriate addition to the "movement." I would train for five weeks, then begin my responsibilities as a fourth-grade teacher in a rural black public school of the Mississippi Delta.

I turned twenty-two on Saturday, graduated from Stanford University Sunday afternoon, and left my family and friends that evening to catch a red-eye to Houston and then a cab that got me to the brick school where I'd teach summer school at eight fifteen in the morning, just slightly late. The neighborhood was a series of projects, the sort of place I'd never been: bleak concrete roadway and rundown brick tenements, the air so humid I could see it shift and turn, distorting everything. It didn't help that I hadn't slept. The room was full of young, bleary-eyed men and women dressed professionally in collared, belted shirts and slacks. The warm air smelled of deodorant and coffee. Everyone stared as I lowered myself to a child's chair with a complaint of plastic. A black woman in a pantsuit resumed speaking where she'd left off, her voice thick with conviction.

"You do not understand the poverty these children come from, their single-parent families. They will bring their circumstances to the classroom, where it is your job to offer them opportunity. You will think you know what they need. You will not."

I had a hard time focusing; I could see the woman's lips moving but found that the words made little sense. It was fine: two years as the issues chair of a multiracial identity and advocacy student organization had taught me all about poverty and inequality, and the consequent struggles of "students of color." This woman cited no statistics or numbers but went on and on about children she'd taught, their situations and their suffering. After the session, I wrote on my evaluation card: "Presentation was lacking in sufficient intellectual content."

· · ·

Promise, Mississippi, population 11,500: the heart of the
Mississippi River Delta, the poorest and blackest part of the
poorest and blackest state in the nation. Although the Delta is some 77 percent black, whites own 95 percent of small
businesses, and most of the cotton that was once picked by
hand was long ago mechanized. Family income in the Delta was $10,000 per year in 2002, and that averaged black
households with white ones. The public schools have been
segregated since 1971: almost all white children attend the
Academy, where scholarships ensure that poor white children don't have to mix with blacks. I found a house to rent in
one of the rare mixed areas, a transitional neighborhood that
was originally all white and was changing as blacks moved in
and whites fled up Highway 82 to gated, upper-class neigh-
borhoods like Mangrove Park, with its cookie-cutter run
of three-story mansions with security guards to police the
fences.

Race in Promise is complex: the White Citizens' Council
began in a house not three blocks from the house I rented.
In a world divided between black and white, I came in an
anomalous middle shade, a mixed-race Japanese-Hawaiian
Russo-Polish Jew who could be Asian, Hispanic, perhaps Es-
kimo or Greek or some other unknown miscegenation; permanent foreignness was no further than the quarter-moon
of my eyes and my gold-brown skin, and nobody around
town seemed to know what to make of me. A couple of children I encountered asked me if I was a "Chinaman," pointing
and exclaiming and chopping their arms about the air; in my
head rose a question I'd once used to frame a panel about at-
titudes of minorities toward other minorities: *What happens
when the "other" meets an/"other"?* I turned to the children
and began speaking with a Monty Python British accent,

thinking I was being clever, not yet recognizing the implications of such difference: there was no such thing as mixed-race Japanese American out here, no such place as Japan, let alone my mother's Oahu or my father's Buffalo and Bay Area.

The whites I encountered, on the other hand, went out of their way to treat me with a sort of racist deference, to assure me they thought of me as practically being white before they alluded to stereotypes about Asians. They often approached to ask, "What are you?" and didn't seem pleased when I replied, "Human. American, even." They shook their heads ruefully when I told them where I worked, as if to say, "You should've known better." Sometimes, they spoke slowly to me, enunciating each word, assuming I might be un-fluent in English. One white grocery store checker asked me, "How's Mohammed's business going down there," imagining that Mohammed, Promise's Persian pawn shop proprietor, must be related to me since neither of us was black or white.

The first day in town, the paunchy, silver-haired realtor gave a warning that I was to hear again and again in different iterations from Delta whites, every time in lowered, earnest voices that strained to ensure I recognized their sincerity and good intentions, that they were letting me in on the truth: "We have heat and we have mosquitoes, but we got nice enough folks here in Mississippi. There's one thing to know about the Delta, though. There's good blacks and bad blacks, and here all the good ones left for the city. What's left—well? Y'all teachers best be careful."

I nodded silently, my face expressionless, a reaction I often found myself forced into in the Delta—how was I to respond to this unsolicited, unabashedly racist advice? I did not know how to recognize boundaries, how to navigate between them from my own undefined middle; from the beginning, I straddled lines.

• • •

Three days before the start of school, I met my assistant principal, Mr. Winston, in his office—he'd reluctantly agreed to come in so that I could set up my classroom. He was a towering, muscular man who must have once been an athlete, his shoulders made broader by a tailored black suit. He stood behind his desk as if keeping it between us. Finally he reached across the desk and offered his hand. "Well, Mr. Copperman. Out here we shake hands like men. I don't know how your people do it."

I took his hand, shook it.

"My people?" I said neutrally. I didn't intend to discuss my cultural background or the merits of the properly masculine Mississippi greeting. Mr. Winston held the grip as if to make a point about his strength, finally released my hand, looked poised to say something more and then thought better of it, and came briskly about the desk.

"Let me show you to your room."

He led the way through the covered walkway toward the squat cinder-block buildings that housed the classrooms. His gait swished his tailored slacks over his fresh-shined shoes. To our right, within the razor-wire fence that circled the school, was the small paved lot I'd parked in.

"The staff parking lot," he said, gesturing at my navy Subaru parked in the space nearest to the office and the white Ford Explorer Winston had pulled up in.

"Park where you can," he said, squaring his feet to face me. "Except that most teachers are considerate and save my space." I looked at the empty parking lot and our two cars, the Explorer glittering blindingly in the sun.

"Sorry, sir. I didn't know."

"I know you didn't," he said, as if he were being charitable, and started off again, the expensive cut of his suit stretched taut across his back. I hurried after him. We passed the first building, then the second, until we reached the third and final hall. Winston felt through his jacket for keys.

"Your hall." He fitted one key and then another in the lock. I glanced at the faded white sign bolted over the door, a koala with a speech bubble declaring: "We won't stop until the Bear Reads!" It seemed a hopeless enterprise, unless koalas had recently demonstrated an unsuspected capacity for literacy. The door, painted pink, had a small wire-reinforced window set in the center, and I could see the long dark run of the hallway inside. I heard a click as Winston found the right key; then he pulled the door open, fumbled on the wall until he found the light switch, and beckoned me inside.

The lights cast a weak yellow glow. The corridor walls had been painted a garish pink, as had the doors, frames, sills, and knobs, but as we neared the end of the hall bigger and bigger patches of the original brown were visible. The floors were clean, but the worn tiles held no shine. The scent of mildew filtered down from mold-marked ceiling panels. Winston stopped at the last door.

"Room 12. Your room. It may not be quite—ready." He fit a key into the lock. The door opened with a squeal of hinges, and Winston stood in the doorway.

"Tomorrow's Sunday, the Lord's day of rest," he said. "But if you have some work you want to do on the classroom, here is your key." He handed me a small iron key, and I slipped it in my pocket. He started away, footsteps echoing the hallway.

"Thank you."

He lifted a hand in acknowledgment. I pushed the door open, stepped inside, and fumbled for the switch. The overhead lights flickered twice and lit the room. "Shit."

The white walls were bare except for green-brown chalkboards and a torn poster that now said "Rea." A metal cabinet lay upended in the back corner, doors gaping open as if gutted. The desks had been pushed into a single brown cluster in the corner opposite the cabinet. Two leaning piles of dog-eared textbooks rose to chest height. I went to the teacher's desk, which sat crooked against the chalkboard, wet my finger, and drew a question mark. Outside I heard the roar of an engine, the rumble of the motor rising and fading. Winston's Ford Explorer.

I brushed the question mark away and opened the desk drawer. Inside lay a single piece of chalk.

The Walmart parking lot at eight p.m. bustled with activity. Trucks with double beds loomed over Chevy sedans with rusting panels and crumpled hoods. People—black and white—directed carts piled high with blue plastic bags through the lot. I found a spot and parked, sat for a moment in the car to observe. The groups were always all white or all black and kept a steady distance, as if bound by invisible strings. The trucks were usually driven by white men, the sedans by black men and women both.

I adjusted the rearview mirror, examined my reflection. I looked harried, exhausted, deep bags under my eyes and my hair drooped from the morning's part into a flat, monkish bowl. I tried to slick it back a bit, rubbed at my eyes, and then gave up on appearances. It was Walmart. I'd come to get supplies.

Inside, the store bustled, people wheeling carts with fast, purposeful strides, cash registers dinging and dinging, while children—white and black—tugged sleeves and raced through aisles. I got a cart and pushed it tentatively through the throngs. Black and white people edged about, careful not to intrude on each other's space, acknowledging one another only to step aside and let a cart past. Only children seemed to notice race, to react—I saw one little black boy of five or six go stiff when he found himself alone in an aisle where a white couple in their thirties were walking, a look of panic seizing his face before he bolted for the free end.

Approaching school supplies, I came on a rack that said, "Back to School Lists!" Printed sheets for each school lay in neat stacks. Booker T. Washington High. Grayson Middle. Promise-Upper Elementary. I hadn't known about this arrangement, was surprised that Walmart was the primary supply source for Promise Schools. I scanned to fourth grade, past Mrs. Akendria Brown, Mrs. Latawna Jackson, Mrs. Dee Williams, and their lists—rulers, protractors, papers, pencils, crayons. At the bottom was "Mr. Michael Copperman," and a single line: "No supply list available." I thought of taking the stack—there were probably thirty sheets left—and writing in a supply list by hand, but it was a lost cause with only two days until the start of school. I set the lists back to the rack. I'd send a list home the first day.

I was keeping my eye out for black children who looked like fourth graders, had noticed a number who seemed the right age. As I stood in the school supplies aisle to buy poster board, a little girl, surely too young for the fourth grade, stood looking at notebooks, talking out loud to herself: "Oooh, this one nice. But it blue which a boy color. This one pink and got little stars, how much it is. Mama say I got three dollars fifty cent to spend. Four dollars! That wrong. These people wrong for that."

I fumbled through my pockets, found fifty cents, walked over by the girl, and pretended to be looking at pens while I set the money on the nearest shelf. "Look at that, somebody left fifty cents!"

The little girl appeared startled.

"How strange!" I smiled at her. "I guess I don't want it. Maybe somebody else might need it."

The girl didn't say anything.

"Would you like the quarters?"

She knit her brow, whispered, "My mama say don't talk to no strangers."

"Your mother's right." I turned down the aisle. When I glanced back she was standing in the same place, still staring at the quarters, though she'd made no move to take them. When I went by the aisle before leaving the store the quarters and the binder with the stars were both gone.

The next morning I woke at six a.m. ready to do what I could. Nobody else was stirring yet that I could see, and there was only the occasional passing car on the highway. The air was already warm but not yet unpleasantly so, and felt drier than during the day. I unlocked the Subaru and stood in the half dark. Out on the highway a six-wheeler rumbled past, safety chains clattering over a pothole. The sun was just rising to the east, a brilliant yellow globe lifting from the flats and edging everything—the walls and roofs, phone poles and parked cars—with gold. I hopped in the car and headed through the dim, still morning for Promise-Upper.

Minutes later, I stood in the middle of the room with wide beams of blinding dawn light slanting through the sooted windows. I'd brought cleaning supplies, trash bags, a broom, a mop, a bucket and rags, but first I needed a clear floor. I grabbed the old stacked hardback books, grunting with the effort, and made piles of them in the corners. There was no air conditioning, and soon sweat ran down my face. The hall was empty, so I stripped to my undershirt. I took the bucket to the boy's bathroom, filled it with yellow-brown water, hauled it back to the room, and mopped once, quickly, to get the worst of the dirt. The water darkened to chocolate. Then I dragged the bucket back, emptied it in the urinal, and refilled it. This time I mopped with even, careful strokes, following the line of the curve to carry the debris, thinking of my father teaching me to mop that way, deliberate and precise, disciplined—he always held that there was a right way to do everything, that what you did was find the courage to choose the correct process.

My entire life, I'd excelled at everything I'd tried through absolute dedication. I grew up a doctor's kid in a sleepy college town with a good public education system, excelled equally in academics and the sport of wrestling through unrelenting hard work, did well enough to gain admittance to Stanford, and worked hard enough there to be accepted to Teach For America. It was only months since I'd left the self-important, technology-driven bustle of the Bay, the stucco and stone towers and Romanesque halls of Stanford—now the Coliseum, now the cabana palace of some expatriate Mexican billionaire, everything palm lined and landscaped, exuding the shine of new money, that crafted California ease: "We don't care about the fourteen digits of our endowment, but have you noticed yonder fresco on the Memorial Church, assembled by artists who painted each tile with porous brushes whose ends were cut from sustainably harvested, naturally regenerating sea sponges? Yes, it's the blond-haired baby Jesus, but notice that the second wise man has an ethnically ambiguous slant to his eyes, and behind him is the African architecture of the 'real' manger, and excuse me, but I have to take a call on my Bluetooth GPS laptop phone." There, even as I'd been an athlete every afternoon at the athletic complex, I'd lived in a co-op and worn tie-dyed T-shirts, had been a leader of an organization advocating census reform and attention to issues of "identity" among mixed-race Asian American students, had published a story with the student literary magazine. At Stanford, on "the Farm," I had taken on an attitude common to those lucky enough to have the privilege of four years of self-exploration in the splendor of material and intellectual paradise: I believed that everything I wanted to accomplish was not only possible but imminent, pending only my own realization of what exactly it was I aspired to do. Teach For America's heady rhetoric of realizing the American dream of equality embodied in the goal "One Day, All Children" didn't sound unrealistically idealistic or grand, but of proper scale given my assessment of my own potential and ability. Of course I could become the change I wanted to see in the world.

When the floors were dry, I hefted the desks across the room and arranged them in rows of four facing the front board, and grinned picturing the desks filled with the expectant faces of children. When the desks were set, I wet the rags and cleaned the teacher's desk and the file cabinet. The cabinet had tape and rust all over the top, and I spent a long time scrubbing and then gave up. Wiping the dusty windowsills, I saw how deep they were and knew where to put the books— now everything had a place.

I went to my car and got three Walmart bags and emptied them on the floor: forty pieces of blue and yellow poster board, ten rolls of adhesive tape, and three packs of permanent markers. I spread sheets of the poster board around me. First, I copied over my class roster to post on the door. Over the names I wrote: "Welcome to Success!" Then I made signs for the classroom: "Together, Yes We Can!" and "There is no CAN'T, only WON'T," and "With WILLPOWER we can do ANYTHING!" I drew smiley faces, stick figures, and pictures of books in the spaces without words, made sign after sign, shaking out my cramped hand. Then I tore squares of adhesive tape and stood on my tiptoes on the wobbly desk chair, teetering. Once the chair tipped and I glanced about the room expecting someone to react, but there was nobody there to see me.

When the last sign was secure, I stood at the front of the room to see what I'd accomplished. There was color now on every wall. Out the windows, the sun had set long ago, and Felicity Street's silhouette of sloping roofs trailed west. A car motored past, throwing the diamond shadow of the fence to the dirt.

I leaned to the wall and sank to the floor. I had a classroom. Now, rest.

Tomorrow, the children.

I wore a suit and tie the first day because I'd heard that formal dress gave you authority, but now I was sweating in the humid air. It was seven thirty in the morning, and most children wouldn't arrive for half an hour. There was a knock on the door. I opened it to find a kind-faced black woman of thirty-five, her hair pulled back into a matronly bun. She was dressed conservatively in a long skirt and high-cut blouse and had a cavernous bag that overflowed with papers and books.

"Hey there," she said, her voice warm and low. "Mrs. Mason, just down the hall. Must be you're Mr. Copperman."

"Yes, ma'am."

She cleared her throat. "Well, Mr. Copperman, I just wanted to welcome you here to Promise-Upper, and see if you need anything before the first day gets going."

"Thanks," I said, thinking of how hard I'd worked the day before, of all my signs and systems that this woman surely couldn't help me with, as I had come up with them myself. "But I can't think of anything I need."

She smiled, nodded at the roster on the door. "Well. I was reading your class list there. You should know you've got some students who could be trouble."

Teach For America emphasizes how important it is not to judge students based on reputation. "I guess I need to find out about the students myself."

"Fair enough," she said. "But honey, if you need help, do feel free to come anytime."

A sudden clamor of children's voices echoed in the hall. We turned. Navy-shirted boys and girls streamed through the hall doors.

"Lord," Mrs. Mason said. "First buses are early. Well, good luck then." She started away.

I watched the children come. So many shades of skin: slate, caramel, coffee. Some were running, others spinning circles, skipping, calling out in eager, insistent voices. One tall, stringy girl flew in front, tossed her backpack in a high arc, turned a cartwheel, and caught the bag just short of Mrs. Mason. When she saw Mrs. Mason, she froze.

"'Scuse me, Mrs. Mason," she said, her eyes exaggeratedly downcast.

"That's OK, baby, just keep your feet on the ground." Mrs. Mason rested her hand on the girl's arm and stepped by.

The girl swung her backpack on. Then she saw me. She was taller than the other children, had white pom-poms in her hair and a proud, angular, fine-boned face with an air of command, as if she claimed every inch of the world around her and dared anyone to tell her differently.

"Wow, man, shoot." The kids behind her stopped, stared, and whispered. I could hear snippets of their conversation:

"... the new man-teacher ..."

"... a real Chinaman ..."

"Bet I'm taller than that little man ..."

"He look like Jackie Chan ..."

"He gone be our teacher?"

"Good morning," I said.

The cartwheel girl narrowed her eyes. "He don't sound like no Chinaman," she said. "They're always like, whaaaaaa—"

"I'm Mr. Copperman," I said. "I teach fourth grade."

They stared at me. Finally, I started for the classroom door. "Jackie Chan, do a karate kick!" a girl hollered.

Further discussion was futile. I closed the door, took a deep breath. I'd have to demand respect—these children didn't know a thing about where I was coming from. A moment later there was a knock. I went to the door. The girl who'd done the cartwheels stood with the children I'd just spoken to.

The girl cleared her throat, a grin tugging at the corner of her mouth. "Um, hi," she said. "We in your class. My name's Talika."

"Hi, Talika." I glanced around her, took in the faces of the students thronging my door. "All of you are in my class?"

They nodded. I took another deep breath, and held the door open.

I was the only male fourth-grade teacher in the district, and only the second male upper-elementary teacher in a faculty of more than thirty, with the only other "man-teacher" a second-year TFA corps member. "We're so glad to have another man," the principal, a kind-faced, gray-haired, immaculately dressed woman named Delia Burtonsen told me when she met me. She had the air of a supercompetent grandmother,

her authority a triumph of black matriarchy—I immediately liked and trusted her, even as she seemed to form an undeservedly high opinion of my abilities in the classroom. The expectation was that as a man, I would necessarily have more authority over the "bad boys" who often terrorize and disrupt even the best-managed classrooms. I doubt that Ms. Burtonsen or anyone else who had read the name "Mr. Copperman" expected a short, ethnically ambiguous, golden-skinned fellow whose students, even in the fourth grade, would often dwarf him.

Still, I was lucky to be placed at Promise-Upper. The staff was dedicated, and the veteran teachers went out of their way to be friendly. The second-year and alumni TFA corps members in my school were supportive, offering to observe and share lesson plans and other resources; they even suggested that we plan together.

Even so, I was dealt a challenge I was unready to meet:

I had twenty-four kids in a fourth-grade class.

All my kids were on free lunch except for two, meaning their families were below the poverty line.

At least two of my kids were repeating the fourth grade, and at least eight had repeated before, meaning many of them were already on a path toward dropping out.

Three-quarters of my kids had failed at least one subject on the Mississippi Curriculum Test (MCT) the year before.

Seven of my students had previously been identified as having serious behavioral problems. Whether so many of them had been placed with me was because I was male was hard to say, but even on paper the group looked difficult.

Five students on my list awaited testing for special education, but that couldn't be done because the district hadn't hired anyone qualified to do the testing. Since it usually took at least six months from testing to get a student into special education, even if I tried I probably wouldn't succeed in getting anyone in until April.

I didn't have enough desks, so some students were forced to sit in free-standing chairs and held folders on their laps.

I didn't have enough social studies textbooks, and the science textbooks wouldn't arrive for months.

Worse than the hand I'd been dealt in resources and students was my own greenness. I began that first week with a behavior system I and three other corps members had devised in Houston teaching seven students at a time. The system was called "Behavior Bucks": students each had a "bank," which was a manila envelope marked with their name, each containing little green bills cut from green construction paper and marked in Sharpie with dollar signs. Behaving badly led to "bankruptcy" and loss of recess and other privileges; each student would manage their own "bank" when they gained money or lost money, walking to the board where the bank envelopes dangled to change their balance. Under close, constant supervision, this system had worked well enough, but now, with my attention divided twenty-four ways amid the frequent chaos of my classroom, runs on the bank were frequent. If I wasn't standing close to the chart and a student went to give him- or herself a reward of a behavior buck or (as was more often the case) to lose a buck, often feeling that loss unfair or undeserved, two dollars or three might make their way into that student's pocket, or none might be subtracted, or dollars might change pockets from one student to another. I lost hours and hours the first week trying to regulate the bank; more often than not, the system that was supposed to help incentivize good behavior led to dispute or an outcome that made no sense, like the entire class losing recess except for three students who were generally quiet and well behaved and who faced now the angry resentment of everyone else. Three days in, I threw the bucks away and introduced a card-color system that most of the other TFA teachers in the school used, my poorly regulated experiment in capitalism done for good.

I had inadequate systems for nearly every part of running a classroom, especially transitions. I got through most days in the classroom itself with students remaining at their desks, and as long as I didn't turn my back most students at least pretended to do their work, although there was an undercurrent of eyes meeting eyes, a stirring that indicated notes being passed. But the moment students began moving, whether for pencil sharpening or paper pickup or bathroom break or lines for lunch or lines for PE, trouble was sure to erupt:

"Man, shoot, somebody pinch me on the neck!" Talika Johnson would call, and turn and kick for the shins of the nearest boy, not really caring if he was the guilty party but looking above all to engage. If I headed in the direction of that problem, three boys would be hitting each other behind me, Charleton would be in the act of tripping Tarvis or gleeking on Tonka, and whispering and giggling would erupt throughout the line. It took me twenty minutes to run a bathroom break, fifteen minutes to get the students to lunch or PE or the computer lab or the library. No journey beyond the classroom walls was without mishap and chaos and the attendant frustration of not being able to finish even simple tasks. The problems soon spread to the classroom itself—Tymedrick might still be angry about something whispered in his ear in line, and he might then knock Kayla's book to the floor intentionally on his way back to his desk. Charleton might snicker, and Kayla glare back at him, and then Charleton might decide to prove something and prepare a spitball to launch the moment I tried to write anything on the board. Each day of the first week got worse; I was getting through half the lessons I'd prepared, often stopping to lecture the class about how they were better than they were acting. I wasn't really teaching so much as disciplining ineffectively.

A matte-black mailbox with "Mr. Copperman" printed on it sat on my desk so that students could let me know what was on their mind. Days in, the mailbox yielded the following messages:

> *Charleton kick me, mr coppertone. He kick me again I gone kill that ugly black boy!—Yours, Kayla*

> *I want be scolar, mr. Coppeman when I be scolar?—Tymdedrick*

> *Melody is a ho!—no name*

> *I kill that boy if he talk 1 more time, mr Copman—Tymedrick*

> *I done not read and spell to good, and I sorry four that—no name*

> *Dear Mr. Chopperman, You the best fourth grade teach i had, you is nice not mean except when you is mad, you try for to teach me learn math reading BFG giants, and you let us play with AtM recess contest but no muesik if we wins. i like have a male man teach me it is nice, thank you. sancerly, Tarvis*

It wasn't clear how many other fourth-grade teachers Tarvis was comparing me to, but this much I knew: he hadn't passed a single subject on the MCT the year before. Still, he had a big, sincere grin, all teeth and crinkled eyes, and a laugh that often led to snorts and brays of mirth. There was nothing but enthusiasm and good nature to him, and though I despaired every time he offered an answer or broke a rule and then made a bigger row still in protesting he hadn't meant to, I couldn't help but like him. His aunty, who was our janitor, pledged to "mind him of God"; I trusted he would need a lot of reminding.

I've never been religious and remained skeptical about the daily "One Nation, under God" that the state mandated I say each morning in reciting the Pledge of Allegiance. Yet on the black side of Promise, every family was Southern Baptist. The first day I watched as other teachers around me began lunch with a prayer, and my kids waited patiently for me to say mine so they could start. Finally I asked my kids to join hands and bow their heads, took a deep breath, and intoned, "Bless our lives, and bless the bounty that we are thankful to have here, dear, um, Lord God Jesus, Amen." The kids repeated the Amen and went after their plates, and so each day I repeated an impromptu prayer to a Lord I wasn't so sure existed at all with a sort of sincerity I'd never known before. Two months earlier I'd been wearing ripped jeans, Birkenstock sandals, and a collared shirt unbuttoned to the navel, lounging on a Stanford balcony with a bottle of wine bloviating about the nature of the universe and the ways to right all ills. Now, I wore a tie, dress shirt, pleated khakis, and patent leather shoes, and I solemnly invoked the grace of the Lord before I tucked myself down on a short lunchroom stool and shared my fourth graders' fried catfish and okra.

After school at the end of the first week, Mrs. Mason tapped me on the shoulder. "How were things so far, Mr. Copperman?"

I blinked. "They were—fine." They were not really fine—children ignored my directions, called out, spoke over my lessons, threw spitballs and paper airplanes, and seemed generally disinclined to heed my directives without argument or objection. But I wasn't going to admit my failures to Mrs. Mason.

"All right, then," she said as if she didn't believe me for a moment and saw the futility in asking me to admit otherwise. "Well, come on now. We gone be late for the welcome."

"Welcome?"

"The raffle, and Dr. Randall gone speak." I followed Mrs. Mason down the hall. We crossed the corridor to the lower school and pushed into a crowd of teachers, mostly women with strong loud voices they all seemed to be using at once.

Mrs. Mason clicked her tongue. "Teachers from the high school." Everyone was dressed like they were bound for church, clothes pinching a little at the waist and neck as if they'd gained a few pounds since the last time they'd worn the garments.

"Come on," Mrs. Mason said. "Let's get seats."

We snaked our way through the crowd, passing the lower school's office, then the doors to the cafeteria. The adult bodies and voices were too big for the space, and their fruity lotions and colognes baked with a lingering hint of grease to make a floral meat pie. Mrs. Mason waved and called names. "Mrs. J. D. Jackson, don't you look fine. Mr. Carpenter. Ms. Darnell, that one fine looking skirt." I was grateful she was leading the way. She reached the end of a row of blue and red children's chairs and motioned for me to sit.

On the low stage in front stood two rows of chairs. Four middle-aged white men stood about the front row of chairs, plaid shirts belted into khaki pants, hands thrust in their pockets. Behind the seats, three black men were deep in conversation. All were graying at the temples, their distinguished air enhanced by black suits with white handkerchiefs spilling from the pockets. Mrs. Burtonsen stood behind them in animated conversation with the superintendent, Dr. Falk, her hand to the woman's arm. Assistant Principal Winston stood beside them but ignored their conversation, his gaze casting about the room.

Mrs. Mason leaned in. "This is how they do the District welcome. The superintendent gone speak, then the Chamber of Commerce raffles off the goodies. All of us are in the raffle pool." She handed me a folded program printed on computer paper. Inside, in a stylized font, were three lines:

Mr. Winston: Introductions and Remarks.
Superintendent Falk.
Raffle, Thanks Chamber of Commerce!

Onstage, the white men moved to the front seats and sat, then the black men took seats behind them. The room settled with a single groan of metal and plastic. Mr. Winston strode to the microphone and beamed at the crowd. "Teachers," he said in incantatory tone, "Secretariat, Librarians, and Staff, Principals Jackson and Crawford, Superintendent Martin, and Gentleman of the Promise Chamber of Commerce: Welcome!"

All about me, people applauded. I clapped too, trying not to smile about "Secretariat." Winston continued. "Today, let us give thanks to God for embarking us on our mission to educate our blessed children. Let us pray we have the strength, the fortitude, the aptitude, and forthrightness to proceed. To succeed. To persevere."

As applause swelled again, Mrs. Mason leaned in. "Nothing that man loves more than the sound of his own voice."

Mr. Winston kept on. Platitudes proliferated. God and Jesus were invoked, the evils of ignorance revoked. The sea of programs waved as sweat trickled down my neck. Finally the superintendent spoke, a tall, dignified woman with her hair pulled back in a tight bun. She gave a short, unmemorable speech on the importance of remembering what was important. The applause was deafening in appreciation of her brevity.

Then the four men from the Board of Commerce stood in unison. The crowd stirred in their seats. A portly, round-faced, silver-haired fellow went to the microphone, detached it, and wet his lips, regarding the crowd with an assurance that suggested he'd done this before. "I suppose we oughta get this show on the road," he said.

People stood and clapped.

"On behalf of the Promise Chamber of Commerce, myself, Mr. Bobby Kirk of the Good Hope Cotton Company, and the Fischers of the Promise Pride Catfish Company—let me say, for all of us, we do appreciate you."

Another city councilman brought a bucket to Mr. Kirk and held it up to show that it was filled with white slips of paper, while the other two men brought boxes, set them to one side, and stood facing the crowd, hands clasped behind their backs.

"Our first prize for tonight is a gift certificate to Walmart for forty dollars."

A murmur of anticipation passed through the room.

Mr. Kirk made a show of reaching in and fishing about

for a slip of paper, which he waved in the air before reading. "Mrs. Lashawnda Johnson."

A woman behind us squealed with pleasure, and people stood to let her reach the aisle. It took a while for her to reach the stage, where Mr. Kirk shook her hand and passed off the prize. Holding the certificate aloft, she made her way back to her seat. I began to pray I wouldn't be given anything. Sweating at the microphone, Mr. Kirk milked each prize. A lawnmower from Delta Hardware went to a man Mrs. Mason informed me was a bus driver; a cosmetics gift pack from Walmart went to a teacher from the lower school; a dozen frozen catfish fillets from Promise Pride went to a member of the "Secretariat."

Then Mr. Kirk held up a square white block. "And now, a brick of fresh-milled cotton from—yes, it is, Good Hope Cotton Company," he said to a smattering of polite applause. I glanced about me for signs that anyone thought this gift inappropriate in the burden of its history, and found none.

Mr. Kirk wiped sweat from his brow and drew a name. "Mr. Harry Winston."

The room fell silent: Assistant Principal Winston at the whim of the lottery was spectacle, all the swagger of his exalted position cut from under him. He stood slowly from his chair and walked for the front with a straight back. At the microphone, he towered over Bobby Kirk. Mr. Kirk looked up at him with an appraising eye, grinned, and offered the cotton.

Winston took the white package, shook Mr. Kirk's hand, and returned to his seat. His chair squealed as it took his weight. I watched him examine the block of cotton, wipe beads of sweat from his brow with his sport-jacket sleeve, and then raise the cotton in front of him as if its meaning might then become clear. For the rest of the raffle, Mr. Winston turned the block of cotton in his brown hands, and sitting there in my own child's chair, I imagined I recognized how history suffused the auditorium and the moment; I thought I stood outside it all looking on. I didn't realize I was as bound by the past as Mr. Kirk and the Chamber of Commerce and the staff of the school and the railroad tracks and the town they split and every boll of cotton in the entire Delta—I didn't know that I was implicated by witness. The pity I felt for Mr. Winston ought to have been for myself for pretending I stood apart from the world.

I found out soon enough.

Driving toward Rosewood that first weekend, the shade down to block the late-day sun, I blinked and found myself in snow. It wasn't snow, of course, but it was white and lay in thick drifts along the side of the road, hiding the dark Delta soil. It covered the road and ditch and fields, even formed a soggy veneer over the beveled banks of the ponds that here and there broke the unrelenting flats.

Cotton.

The pickup ahead of me kicked white clouds from the road that turned circles against the blue sky until the real clouds and the clouds of cotton were indistinguishable. I had the windows closed and the air conditioning cranked, and this suddenly white world was new and unsullied. I pressed the pedal to the floor, bound faster and farther and surely toward some purer end, the clouds of white drifting over the highway, burying and baptizing with every mile.

CLASSROOM MANAGEMENT

On a blinding October afternoon, Assistant Principal Winston met me in his office. He again kept his desk between us.

"Son, what's your approach to classroom management?" He bared his teeth when he spoke, seemed perpetually about to say something simultaneously cruel and amusing. I wasn't sure about being called son, baby-faced as I was, by a man also in his twenties, but there seemed little choice but to accept his terms of address. I thought about how to answer the question. According to the notebook we received in training, classroom management cannot be separated from student interest. Children who were learning behaved well. Children not learning behaved poorly. Teach well, and you'd succeed, for, as one particularly inspired passage had noted, "children incline toward the light." I wanted to be prepared and had read the materials several times.

"Sir, it's my philosophy that good teaching is good management."

"Well," Winston said. "There's other philosophies." He slid open a drawer in his desk and pulled free a paddle, three feet and laminate, a slim handle and a long, flat striking surface. He whistled it through the air and struck the desk with a crack. Then he handed it to me. Its solid, balanced weight made you want to swing it despite its purpose. We had been warned during orientation that we might encounter corporal punishment, that it was still common in the Delta, even "culturally appropriate." One TFA teacher who had stayed past her two years, who'd been here five years now and adopted a Southern lilt even though she was originally from Maine, had said, "These days, I just send them to get whupped good if that's what it takes to make them behave," and I had shaken my head at her callous zeal for such abuse. When one of my college friends who was concerned with human rights had found out that I was headed to the Delta, he sent me an investigative report on corporal punishment in Mississippi that condemned it as appallingly violent.

"Hope you won't need this for my students," I said, grinning to suggest a joke.

Winston met my eyes, spoke with disturbing intensity. "I do not spare the rod."

In the first weeks of school I committed to a strategy of parent contact, a lynchpin of good classroom management, according the manual. I called every student's home once a week, sometimes several times, hoping to create a web of accountability, to give kids the sense that everyone around them insisted on their best effort. The suggested strategy was to avoid only calling home when students behaved poorly—it was essential to validate good behavior too, so that students associated the teacher with positive consequences. I liked this idea, pictured students beaming with pride as their parents spoke my name into the phone.

In practice, however, this strategy was hard to execute. So many students were behaving poorly that there were no purely positive calls. Many parents were skeptical if I claimed that their child had done well, imagining I was holding something back.

"That don't sound like the boy at all," Tarvis's grandmother said when I finally reached her. "That devil-child ain't done no right since he was born. You sure you got the right boy?"

Other parents stopped taking my calls. "Why is you gone

waste my time talking bout this child done right?" asked an impatient mother when I called a bit late on a Friday night before hanging up the line. Often, I reached a younger or older sibling or grandparent. I stopped asking to speak to the father; there were few fathers.

"Mama already asleep, but I can take a message," Melody's thirteen-year-old sister told me at six in the evening.

"I'm glad you called, but I can't do nothing with that boy. He's too big for me to whup," Tymedrick's grandmother said.

"Why you keep calling us when the problem is you can't get them children to mind they manners?" said Irvin's seventeen-year-old brother before hanging up the phone.

One student, Antiquarian Herring, actually ordered me not to call. "Why you gone call my mama?" he said in class; and later, with clenched fists, "Don't call my mama no more!"

Antiquarian was a special case. Thin shouldered and sharp chinned, with great dark eyes, he had a furtive and twitchy manner, was prone to fits. Some mornings he refused to do work, would at the slightest insult leap from his seat with clenched fists to fight whoever was meddling him. "I gone kill that big-mouth girl Talika, she say more bout my mama," he'd say, straining against my grip as Talika smiled. He had a habit of glancing nervously over his shoulder. Whenever I disciplined him, gave even a gentle request to get to work, he'd lock his jaw and cross his arms, shake with defiance. I praised him for anything I could—his work was so poor it was difficult to find anything he'd done well, so I gave him classroom tasks like sweeping the room and cleaning the boards, complimented him on his efficiency. He looked suspicious at first but took pride in the work, even stayed after school to complete special tasks. He wet paper towels and wiped the dusty corners where the broom wouldn't pull; he shone the desks until they glowed. He seemed to enjoy the single-mindedness of work, would look disappointed for a moment when he finished and was again in a world without immediate purpose.

Antiquarian excelled on the kickball field at recess, loved the game and being out on the grass field in the sunlight. He went from child to child during lunch and insisted that they hurry, that they'd eat through our time; when we reached the field and I let the children free, he sprinted off bellowing and whooping, turning cartwheels and backflips like a tiny, crazed gymnast. He was everywhere on the field, diving for catches, turning singles into doubles, triples into home runs. I played sometimes with the children, high school soccer useful now, and Antiquarian became excited about my skill. "Man, shoot, Mr. Copperman, you can *play!*" he'd say. I showed him how to kick with the flat of his foot instead of toeing the ball, how it gave you a measure of control. I used the threat of losing kickball to keep his behavior in line—and it worked. I called Antiquarian's home every night wanting to report his success—how polite he'd been that day, how he'd stayed after school to vacuum the reading rug and mop the floors. I never reached anyone, and his mother had no message machine, but I was determined to connect with her, to do whatever it took.

One afternoon, the secretary appeared at my door and told me that Mr. Winston wanted to see me and Antiquarian in the office—she'd watch the class. Baffled, I went. Mr. Winston was filling in for Mrs. Burtonsen, who was out for eight weeks after surgery. I tried to put my hand to the boy's shoulder as we walked, but he flinched from my touch.

In the principal's office, an old woman with carved cheeks and white, wispy hair glared from a corner. Antiquarian hurried to her, and she cradled him to her, a protective arm about his chest. Winston eyed me as if he'd confirmed some tawdry hunch about me. "This is Antiquarian's grandmother, Mr. Copperman. Please, go on and tell Mr. Copperman what you told me," he said.

"Sir, you got to stop calling the boy's mama," she said. "Ain't you got no heart or sense? Don't you care bout what happen to him?"

I must have looked astonished, for Mr. Winston cut in. "The boy's mother has caller ID and has seen that you've called quite a bit."

I nodded. "I have. Nearly every night."

"And why were you calling every night?" Winston narrowed his eyes with confusion.

"I was just trying to talk to her about Antiquarian's behavior."

The grandmother cut in. "But the boy say he been good, that he ain't been in no trouble."

I smiled at Antiquarian. "That's right. He's made great improvement. I was calling to explain just how good he's been, how well he's doing. I never reached her."

The grandmother looked horrified. "So the boy ain't been bad?"

"A few times. But mostly, I was just trying to—communicate."

She sighed. "Lord." She put her hand on Antiquarian's arm. "Go on and pull up that shirt, baby, and turn around."

Antiquarian reluctantly turned and lifted his shirt. His wiry back was cut, was crossed with welts of pink and red and purple, scabbed blue-black with white wells of pus, and elsewhere slashed to open, angry flaps. I winced.

Winston spoke. "It's my understanding that the boy's mother, who works evenings out at Parchman Prison, has taken up with a guard out there. He has a mind that the boy needs discipline. When the couple would return home at midnight and see your number on the caller ID, well, they assumed—"

"With a fan belt," the grandmother said quietly. "A fan belt. On a little boy like that. Night after night."

She and Winston stared at me. Antiquarian let his shirt fall and turned with pleading eyes. "Tyrone say if I don't mind my teacher, them po-pos gone take me away to Parchman, put me in a dark cell so I ain't never gone see daylight. He say he got to learn me so I can learn."

"But—" I began, looked at Antiquarian's clenched jaw. What had I done? "I just wanted them to know you were trying."

Winston spoke slowly, a hint of a smile on his lips. "You must mind your teacher, son. But I believe this will be the end of Tyrone's—*assistance*—with Mr. Copperman's discipline."

When we were out of the office and back on the hall, I stopped, turned to the boy. "I'm so sorry, Antiquarian."

He stared at the ground. "I been asked you not to call my mama, and you didn't care."

"I didn't—I didn't know."

He looked at me. "You was calling my mama to say I did good?"

I nodded. "You've done great. You're making progress, and soon you'll be one of the best students in the class. In the whole school."

The words sounded thin.

"I just want to play kickball." This admission seemed to get to him, and he looked at the ground, sniffled and blew his nose on his sleeve, shook his head. "Don't worry, Mr. Copperman. It don't matter what you do, good or bad, right or wrong. It don't matter."

I thought of his mother's boyfriend, the fan belt cutting already abraded flesh, night after night these weeks Antiquarian had done as I'd asked. All for twenty minutes on the kickball field, under the open sky. "It matters, Antiquarian."

He looked past me, down the dim hall to the square window bright with sunlight. "If you say so, Mr. Copperman. You the teacher."

I was the teacher. I went home every day that week and tried to remember what I'd come to do: offer opportunity and inspiration and change. I thought of finding Tyrone and taking a fan belt to him; I thought of going back to Winston and protesting that this wasn't my damn fault, that I'd meant well, and what was the difference anyway between his paddle and Tyrone's fan belt? I thought of how, finally, all my anger sought to deflect guilt that was mine alone—I had done this to Antiquarian—and if I accepted it, I had two choices: I could quit and leave my classroom without a teacher, like the fifth-grade class on the next hall where Mr. Brooks, a man with a Delta High School education, was a "permanent substitute" who made no attempt at instruction, patrolling the aisles with a yardstick, forcing the misbehaving to get in pushup position and stay there until he said they could return to their seat. I could leave my classroom to that fate, or I could accept what I'd done and do better.

I was determined to make it up to Antiquarian, to prove to him that making good choices mattered. The next week I wrote a series of stories for the class's guided reading group that featured Antiquarian as the hero, a "young, strong boy with great skill in the game of kickball and sharp mind." In the story, a fictional class taught by a "Mr. Coppertes" in Room 12 at Stanford-Upper Elementary faced a series of crises grounded in events from class—invasions by a plague of monster cockroaches, a stifling heat wave and no air conditioning, a kickball launched beyond a field's fence and lost. Only Antiquarian could solve each problem, which snowballed into a dilemma that required intelligence and pluck: the cockroaches were defeated by special traps created from a mastery of acute and obtuse angles folded from paper; the heat wave was beaten back by cleverly covering the windows of the classroom with students' jackets and writing a story about icy popsicles so vivid that every student was chilled to the bone. Other stories contained a moral dimension: the hero went beyond the fence in search of the kickball and found another kickball that wasn't his but would do. His decision to seek out the owner yielded not only the original ball but also the gift of a car from a rich, kickball-loving car dealer.

Antiquarian liked that story a great deal, and as he finished reading it his hand waved in the air. I went to him at his desk and leaned over him. "Yes?"

"What the car was, Mr. Copperman? It were a Cadillac on 22s, weren't it? A white Caddy rolling on 22s!"

Although the misconjugated past tense and spinning rims on Cadillacs were not exactly the lesson I was trying to teach, I was pleased enough with his enthusiasm to smile, clap him on the shoulder, and say, "Yes. Yes, for Antiquarian's good choices and honesty, I believe it was a white Cadillac with 22s. I believe that's exactly right."

The school had arranged a field trip to the Choctaw mounds and cultural museum outside Rosewood to coincide with our social studies unit concerning Mississippi Native history. We'd come up with full funding—all the children had to do was get a permission slip signed. Antiquarian kept shrugging when I asked him about the slip, and so I told him how the

Choctaw had made high ground from the swampy flats, how over generations they'd built height until their hills were a hundred feet high and they could spot anyone coming from a mile off. Antiquarian had his eyes closed, apparently picturing such elevation. He blinked them open and looked at me. "Mr. Copperman, what it like to stand up on a mountain?"

"On a mountain?" I said, thinking he'd missed my point.

"A hill. Whatever. I ain't never been up on anything," he said.

I looked at him, imagining the view from the snow-topped Sierras I'd backpacked as a boy, and kept the incredulity off my face as I realized it could be true: there were no hills in Triangle County. "It's amazing how far you can see from up high," I said.

"I want to see," he said, his brow furrowed as he pictured it. "Grandmom say I'm part Choctaw anyhow—her grandmom were."

I grinned. "Well, then. Get that slip signed."

On the way to Rosewood, Antiquarian sat next to me in the window seat—I was determined to keep him from the back of the bus, where he might get to fighting with the other boys and ruin his trip. He kept his face pressed to the glass the entire trip, watching the cotton fields flash past in blocks of white and brown, pointing to flashy cars as we came to Rosewood proper and then howling with delight as we came to the Choctaw museum and he saw for the first time the grassy hill lift from the brown plain, the small round museum at the crest like a landlocked lighthouse. In the parking lot outside the museum, the children chattered brightly, pointing at the cars on the roadway below, the novelty of the world from a higher vantage. Antiquarian was unusually subdued, staring about with an overwhelmed awe, as if afraid the ground would slip from beneath his feet. A stern-faced white woman of about sixty walked out of the front entrance with quick, small steps, looked at the four buses and all the children, and did an about-face and walked briskly back inside. Ten minutes later she came out and crooked a commanding finger at me and the rest of the teachers; we told the students to be still and went to meet her, glancing over our shoulders to make sure no antics ensued.

"Greetings y'all," she said. "Ms. Dotson. We can only take one class at a time, so y'all will need to wait out front until I come and get you. Five minutes for a group is all we can do. Please keep the children quiet, and do not let them touch the artifacts."

Before any of us could respond, Ms. Dotson was gone; I saw Ms. Hutchinson and Ms. Beadle glance at each other and roll their eyes. We returned to our classes, and Ms. Hutchinson's class was beckoned in from the door. We were the last bus, and so with a sigh I went back to the class to wait, knowing the children's impatience would only grow. When Talika saw the second class go in she threw up her arms in disgust. "Man, shoot, Mr. Copperman. Why we got to be last?"

"Someone has to go last," I said.

Antiquarian looked more hurt than outraged. "But Mr. C, why do it have to be *us*?"

To get the children to wait, I commenced a game of vocabulary telephone, where I whispered a sentence containing one of the week's vocabulary words and then the class tried to see if the last student in line could retain the right sentence. The game required relative silence, and the class wanted badly to beat me, though they couldn't manage it: "The girl was filled with sadness" became "The gull was full of sand"; "Funerals are often mournful" became "Guns all sound powerful"; and "Patience is always rewarded" was on its way to becoming something equally inaccurate when Ms. Dotson finally crooked her summoning finger. I quieted the children and led them to the front, placing a calming hand on Antiquarian's shoulder as he danced from foot to foot.

Ms. Dotson stood before us at the glass entrance door as if to physically prevent us from entering. She showed her teeth in an unconvincing smile. "Welcome, children, to the Choctaw Native American Museum. The Choctaw made this mound long before any of us—of you—ever came to Mississippi. They lived here, which is why we call them NATIVE Americans."

I heard a giggle, saw Talika laughing at the woman's exaggerated manner, and glared at her as she covered her mouth with both hands to quell her laughter.

"Today you will see some of their things that they left behind," she said. "You may look, but you MAY NOT touch. Please keep your voices low."

She pushed through the door and disappeared inside. I turned to the class. "Be on your best behavior."

Talika spoke up. "Why she gone talk to us like we stupid?"

I shook my head. "She was just telling you the rules," I said. "Now. Let's go see."

Inside, the room was dimly lit, and a half-dozen open cases contained headdresses, arrowheads, pouches, beads, and stoneware. On the walls were stylized pictures of Choctaw warriors standing with raised spears, glowering down on a grassy plain. Antiquarian pointed. "Oohwee, Mr. C! They *bad.*"

I smiled at him. The children dispersed throughout the room, and I wandered with them, keeping my eye on Ms. Dotson, who stood with crossed arms, lips pursed in discomfort. Antiquarian had paused by a case of chipped-obsidian knives with long, smooth bone handles. He pointed at the long blade. "That's something, huh, Mr. C?"

I smiled and nodded. The collection was haphazard and randomly arranged, but the children didn't know the difference. I went for a moment to a group of girls who were admiring the beadwork on a pouch, and turned only when it was too late.

"Get your hands out of there!"

Ms. Dotson stood over Antiquarian, her hand cinched about his wrist; he was struggling to pull it back.

"Let go! Let go!" he yelled.

I moved quickly to them, took Antiquarian's hand and then put my hand to Ms. Dotson's until she released him and he went still and silent. "Easy."

"He was touching that knife," she said, pointing at the obsidian blade.

"Antiquarian?" I said.

"I had just wanted to see if it was sharp," he said, staring at the floor and digging his toe into the tile.

"I told you, DO NOT TOUCH!" She looked around the room, where all the children were watching, then back at Antiquarian. She bent over him as I held him, leaned close. "These—*terrors*—can't follow directions. That's the last time. We're ending the tours to the public schools."

I pulled Antiquarian back, away from Ms. Dotson, and spoke softly. "Ma'am," I said. "They're children. Children make mistakes. I'm very sorry."

She frowned, cocked her head a little in my direction. "Well. I never knew the Orientals were in league with these—*kind*."

I felt my face flush, bit my lip and looked about the room at the faces of my children. "Well, ma'am," I said, pointing at the door for the children to form a line, "it seems to me that except for—*folks*, like you, we're all in it together." I turned my back and guided Antiquarian out the door, pausing for a moment before boarding the bus to gaze down at the rooftops and cars made small from this temporary height.

A week later, Antiquarian started it. I'd been up until one a.m. the morning before preparing the lesson, and I was excited about it, but the children were listless and disinterested. I called on Antiquarian because his eyes had a glazed look. "Antiquarian!"

He returned from whatever dream he'd been in, and said, "Woof?"

A few boys in the back made whispered woofs of their own; Antiquarian's face turned red. "Sorry, Mr. Copperman," he said.

From the back, someone mewled, then crowed. "Stop!" I said.

And it did, for the moment—until I started the lesson. Now a gorilla grunted, a cat purred, and we were done with my teaching strategy for acute and right angles. It wasn't any one child, but many. Antiquarian held his hands to his mouth to keep in the laughter. I faced them, hoots and howls filling the room, and broke the chalk in my hand. When I erased the recess minutes they'd earned, calls of protest blended with the animal noises.

I rang my bell and the room went silent, and I spoke in a quiet, tight voice: "There will be no more of this." The children's eyes widened with my intensity—months and months now I'd been working for them, and now here they were, unappreciative, unwilling to learn. The quiet held for a moment. Then a single bark came from the back of the room. I slammed my palm to the desk so loudly that Talika nearly fell from her desk. Then I reached to the stack of office referrals and began to write, glancing up with a danger that kept them silent. I wrote ten referrals, the pencil cutting to the desk; I sent every child who could have made the menagerie. I sent Antiquarian, too—he'd started it, and thought it funny. If they got licks, they deserved it.

Ten minutes later, Assistant Principal Winston was at my door with the line of boys in tow, paddle in hand. "Some problems in the classroom today?"

"Yes, sir."

"These boys were acting the fool?"

I nodded.

He leaned from the waist and clapped me—cuffed me, nearly—on the shoulder. "Since discipline has gone, let me return it."

He unbuttoned his jacket and slid it off, pit stains beneath his arms, tie askew. He held out the coat; I took it. He ran a caressing hand up and down the length of the paddle. "How did this start?"

Talika thrust up her hand.

"Yes, Ms. Johnson," Winston said.

She smiled sweetly. "It was that boy Antiquarian making a barking noise."

Winston eyed the line of them, picked Antiquarian out. "Is that true, son?"

Antiquarian lowered his head.

Winston cocked his head toward the board. "Hands to the wall," he said. "Go on, now." He adjusted his grip on the handle. An anticipatory shiver ran the back of my neck.

Winston looked to me and said, "Now, boy, learn to mind your teacher."

He swung, a blurred arc and a solid, thick crack of contact. I winced.

Antiquarian didn't flinch.

"Hands to the board," Winston said, pushing the boy to the wall, though Antiquarian hadn't moved. A vein throbbed in his thick neck; a single thread of sweat ran from his forehead to his jaw. He set himself again. Winston looked to me again and smiled. "If you act like animals, we'll treat you like animals. Now, mind your teacher, boy." He swung from the hips with a batter's break to the wrist, the whirr through the air and the snap of wood to flesh startlingly athletic.

Antiquarian's lip twitched with the force of the strike, and a trail of mucus came from his nose. His expression didn't change.

"Hands to board!" Winston said. "You gone learn, or I gone learn you better."

Each blow, Winston swung harder, and Antiquarian grew calmer. He seemed to welcome each strike, as if here, in punishment, was a place he was most comfortable. It wasn't that the blows weren't painful: when the second boy came up, he let out a scream and began to blubber, and later, to choke on his own phlegm.

It took pain to keep standing there—I shoved my thumbnail through the skin of my index finger, stained my khakis with blood. I don't remember the wounds, just the begging of children, the whistle of Winston's swing.

A hundred licks.

Here I was, found now in the fall of a paddle, the snap of wood to flesh and a child's cry. When Winston was finished, he took back his jacket, slid it on, and took my hand and drew me close, pounded my back as if we were brothers or teammates. His palm was wet, sweaty from the paddle. I said nothing, could neither push him away nor accept his embrace. When Winston was gone and the children were back in their seats I turned to the chalkboard. The surface was wet with tears and snot wiped from the boys' hands, and the lesson was still there, angles and letters smeared to broken lines and malformed shapes, like some new and terrible language.

The children had to go to PE, and so I walked them to the gym. Antiquarian was last in line, and he turned to me as the children filed in. His body shook, but he didn't say a word, just stared with as pure a hatred as I've ever seen.

I watched with guilty eyes until he was inside. I was glad when he was gone—it was a relief to have him out of sight.

I made my way out the school gates on foot. We weren't supposed to leave the school grounds, but I couldn't care. I turned on Felicity Street and walked. It was hot, the air dry and still. I'd never known the smell of these streets—the school was kept clean, the litter cleared each afternoon and the concrete hosed down each Friday. That air smelled like dried grass and bodies and dust. Felicity in this sun had a baser reek: diapers folded and left on the roadway baked and baked in the sun. Garbage piled in front yards. At a corner, a package of raw chicken gone bad, a twisting of maggots at the wet center and the edges dried. Three mangy dogs fought for the right to eat it, flies circling about them as they turned and bent for each other's necks. Three men in yellowed undershirts egged them on; it seemed they might have bet on the winner, or at least, it seemed to matter that the battle persisted. They eyed me but had no attention to spare, as one dog got a bite on another's stringy leg. The victim screamed, an urgent keening. The whole world stood by and enjoyed the suffering. I felt bile rise in my throat, bent over a fence and hocked and spit into a yard.

"Oh, no, you didn't," I heard a female voice call. I wiped my mouth and met the judging eyes of a white-haired woman sitting in the weak shade of a porch on a couch that sank to the ground at the middle.

"Sorry."

"You gone clean that up?"

I looked into the dirt yard, a scatter of cans and cardboard the only decoration.

"Well?"

There was no place to hide the spit, and soon enough it would sink into the dirt. I wasn't going to do anything. I turned my eyes to the road and walked away, the woman hollering something at my back that had to do with China and her fitting to beat my yellow ass. The fence lines queued but never met. The dog cried and cried behind me; the men bellowed encouragement; I continued until the keening was only an echo in my ears. Now I came on two teenage boys fighting in the street, throwing punches from the hips, the muscles of their shoulders and arms rippling as they turned circles on the dusty road. One boy caught his feet, fell cursing, and the other boy jumped on him throwing blow after blow, the boy on the ground cowering with his hands about his head. He was going to be hurt. With a cry I charged in, grabbed the boy on top about the chest and tore him off. He twisted in my arms, finally threw me off with a yell. "Get off me!" he yelled, spinning away. "Get off me!"

I turned to the boy on the ground, who'd sat up. "Are you all right?"

Eyeing me warily, the boy stood and brushed his hands on the back of his pants. He was unmarked except a little dirt on his cheek. "We was just—playing."

They backed away together, turned and jogged to put some distance between us. "Crazy fucking Chinaman," one boy muttered. Fifty yards down the road the boys stopped, turned to one another. The boy who'd fallen flexed his arms and popped his neck, lowered his chin and lifted clenched fists. Then they began again to circle, a dance of steps and harmless blows, voices echoing along the asphalt.

I would like to say that I returned from that walk down Felicity and protested, that I reported Assistant Principal Winston to Mrs. Burtonsen when she returned or lodged a complaint with the district or the state. I would like to say that I told anyone at all. I would like to say that I found a way to make it up to Antiquarian, that I was kind to him; I would like to tell a story about how both of us were redeemed, how we finally stood together against an unfair world. I would at least like to say that I never again sent a child to the office knowing they were going to be paddled. But I had to get up the next day and teach, and the next day after that, and I believed that the ends justified the means, that if I didn't teach well I was failing those children. I thought I had no choice.

The days I was forced to send children to the office and I knew Assistant Principal Winston was on duty, I comforted myself with the studies that say that corporal punishment, if calmly and fairly applied, is as effective as other means of punishment. Many of us teaching in the Delta discussed the study, repeated its findings in what now seems a strange circle of denial: we thought we wanted to be justified in participating in a system where children were routinely beaten. Really, we were overwhelmed; what we wanted was to be forgiven. I told myself that sending children to be paddled was necessity, but, somewhere buried, I knew it was indefensible.

As for Antiquarian, I had taught him that the world was unjust, its spoils going to the bully with the biggest stick; once taught, some lessons can't easily be corrected. Every time I saw him I was reminded of what I had done, which I did not want to remember or didn't know how to face, and so I kept my head down and persisted, pretending that nothing had happened at all. I avoided him as best I could, never said his name or looked his way for fear the shame would fill me anew. One day after school, I noticed his green camouflage jacket still hanging on a hook, and I found I couldn't remember if he had even been there. The jacket was still there the next morning and afternoon and the days and weeks after, and Antiquarian was not. Eventually word came from the office that he had moved to Memphis with his mother and stepfather. Only months later did I hear the rumors from the children about how he was in juvenile hall now, the story being that he woke late one night after arguing with a cousin earlier in the day who was staying at his apartment. He rose, found his baseball bat, and delivered nearly a dozen blows to the boy's head while the boy screamed and begged. Here is what I imagine some nights when I try to sleep, and conscience harries me in the turning dark: that each time, before Antiquarian swung again on his helpless victim, he chanted, "Now you gone *learn*!"

WHAT YOU CAN GIVE

At first, I didn't know that Tevin would be a problem. Amid the tumult and clamor of my classroom, he didn't draw attention, a slim, handsome boy with long arms and a careful, almost elegant manner. It was his silence that first made me notice him: I asked him a direct question the second day, and he turned and pretended not to have heard. When I pressed, he smiled, bowed his head. When I called roll he'd raise his hand but say nothing, just flash his strange smile, which showed no teeth—the corners of his mouth turned up, but his gray eyes remained implacable and wary. He could speak and sometimes would answer a question with a few words, but mostly he smiled and looked away. It wasn't nervousness, but indirect disobedience: if he didn't care to do something, he ignored what was said, glanced away, and kept on as he liked.

As time wore on, he started to do exactly as he wanted. He wanted to throw spitballs, take other children's pencils and break them, and mock me behind my back. He liked to flick other children behind the ear, pinch them on the soft flesh of the upper arm, gleek saliva onto the back of an unsuspecting neck. He liked to make animal noises, to hoot and whistle and bark. He wrote the word *fuck* a hundred times when asked to write a five-sentence paragraph—complete with five periods and capitals to satisfy the assignment. "This isn't OK," I said, standing above him at his desk with the paper as he grinned unsettlingly and stared at the ceiling. Whenever I caught him and tried to discipline him, he turned his head and smiled infuriatingly, and refused to respond. The first time I sent him to the office, he returned tear streaked, and I knew that

Assistant Principal Winston had given him licks. He stared at me through the rest of class with a disarming intensity.

I called the number for Tevin's home that night. "I'm Jackson Johnson," a gravely black voice said. "The boy stays with me and my daughter Lizy—we foster kids for the state. I'll come on in and speak to you, Mr. Copperman."

The next morning, Tevin walked through the door before the bell, smiling.

"Good morning, Tevin," I said.

He walked to the nearest empty desk and tipped it to the floor with a crash.

"What do you think you're doing?"

He tipped the next desk in the row, then the next. Children in his path fled as he tipped their desks with their papers and folders as well.

"Stop!" I yelled. He met my eyes for a moment and began on the next row. I started for him across the room, and he upended desks in my path and moved toward the door. I pushed desks aside, running now, but he was out the door and down the hall. "Go to the office!"

He turned, leaned so near I could feel his warm breath on my face. Then he jumped toward me. I flinched and stepped back. He grinned, nodded once, and made his way down the hall with a swaggering step that filled me with rage, and for a moment I thought to kick his jaunty feet out from under him. I started after him, then remembered the other children and turned back. In the classroom, everyone was talking at once. Half the desks lay on the floor, tipped on their sides and corners, some upside down with their legs in the air, and folders and papers were scattered across the floor. I quieted the children, set them to putting the desks upright, and called the office on the intercom. "Tevin Downs just turned my classroom upside down," I said when the secretary answered. "Then he ran out."

There was a long, static-filled pause, and the secretary said, "Tevin Downs is here, Mr. Copperman. He just come through the door."

I stood at the intercom. "Huh."

Two hours later, I received a note telling me that Tevin had been sent home. On my free period, I went to the office and knocked at Mr. Winston's door, but he was out and Mrs. Burtonsen was away at a conference in Biloxi. The secretary called me over with a crooked finger and leaned in. "That boy was wearing two pairs of pants," she whispered. "Guess he was grinning at Mr. Winston while he was getting whupped. Mr. Winston, he got worked up. Stomped out of here after Mr. Johnson come in to get the boy."

After school, I sat in the empty classroom, the dull sun of October filtering through the back windows in blocks of heatless light. Winston still hadn't returned. When there was a knock, I thought it might be him and hurried to the door. Outside was a black man of about sixty, his hair gray and white. He leaned to a cane that was too short, his shoulders rounded and bent. "Must be you Mr. Kato," he said. "Mr. Johnson. Tevin stay with me. You'd called yesterday for me to come in, and I thought with what-all today I'd better come in all the same." He smiled, revealing gapped teeth, and extended his free right hand. His grip was firm.

"Sir," I said.

Placing the tip of the cane with each step, he made his way to my desk.

I hurried to pull my chair around so he could sit. Thanking me, he settled to the seat. I went about the desk.

"So," I said.

"Yes, Lord," he said, and chuckled from the belly, deep

laugh lines crinkling at his eyes. He had a kind face. "Guess you wasn't figuring on no boy like this one."

"So—there have been issues before?"

He shook his head. "I only had the boy three weeks—his second or third foster placement in a year. And I'm gone tell you the truth, Mr. Copperman—I don't know how long I can hold on. The boy been nothing but trouble at home, and he too fast for me, what with my leg. I can't catch him for to whup him."

I took all this in. "What do you know about him, his history?"

Mr. Johnson leaned back in his chair and frowned. "That lady from the district, the behavioral specialist, Ms. Watson, she ain't been to see you? She ain't told you nothing?"

I shook my head. I knew the behaviorist by sight only, a reed-thin white woman in her late thirties with a shock of red, frizzy hair and a wardrobe that seemed to consist solely of strangely patterned skirts with matching leggings. A couple days a week she pulled a couple of my problem boys, including Tevin, out from class for "meetings"; they returned grinning, plastic toys and trinkets like yo-yos and playing cards clutched gleefully in hand, boasting about all she was "gone give" them next time. It was my impression that she was bribing them with baubles, but then I wasn't a "specialist."

"Well. I don't know where to start. You better contact them folks. I just need you to know—I told Mr. Winston this too, when he was telling me I'd better not let the boy wear two pants or whatever all—I can't do nothing with him. I done what I can. I tell him this way ain't no way but a bad end. But he don't respect me. He don't respect nothing but a good whupping, and I can't catch him to lay a proper hand on him. He just smile at me and keep on."

I tried to think what to say about "laying a hand on him." "Did his social worker suggest any—other—methods for discipline?"

Mr. Johnson grinned. "Mr. Barker was the one told me a good whupping the only thing the boy respect. You should've seen that man make the boy jump."

I wanted to demand more, looked at him with his hands folded earnestly over the head of his cane. "Thank you for the information," I said.

Later that week, I ran down the behavioral specialist on my break while the children were on PE. "I'm Mr. Copperman, a fourth-grade teacher. Can I speak to you for a moment about Tevin Downs?"

She looked surprised that I was addressing her, smiled, switched her bag and purse to her left hand, and shook my hand. "I'm Ms. Watson, pleased to meet you. Tevin? Oh my, yes, Tevin. He's a special case. Let's get to my office for privacy."

Her office was a small room also used by one of the special ed teachers; in one corner, I saw a box full of the dollar-store toys she gave the boys. She entered, set down her bag, and hurried to her files, rifling through them with such urgency that it seemed she was afraid I might abandon her there if she wasn't quick enough. It occurred to me that perhaps few people here paid her any attention at all, let alone asked her for advice.

"Here we go, now," Ms. Watson said, lifting a manila folder aloft. She took the file, sat down and opened it, paged through its contents, and finally held up a single, typed sheet of paper. "How much do you know, Mr. Copperman?"

I shook my head. "Just that he's in foster care, and his foster-father says he doesn't know how to handle him."

She leaned toward me, lowered her voice to what was almost a whisper. "That ain't the half of it, Mr. Copperman."

What Ms. Watson told me strained credulity. Tevin Downs had been born to an alcoholic, crack-addicted mother in Midnight, Mississippi, where he had spent the first eight years of his life in shelters and tents and boxes on the streets or in the cotton fields. His mother had been unable to identify a father on his birth certificate. He begged and stole to survive, knew no personal hygiene, and had never celebrated a birthday—he did not know how old he was when he was taken as ward of the state. The state felt fine starting him in school from the beginning: his physical development had been so stunted by malnourishment that he was still smaller at around age eight than the average kindergartner. As for his mental status and development, tests proved consistently inconclusive. One report indicated that he had all the signs of fetal alcohol syndrome and retained a number of "permanent, complicating behavioral accommodations to his early environment." An IQ test he'd taken concluded that his intelligence was well above average. His academic records were limited—it seemed that he hadn't, in fact, ever completed a full grade due to disciplinary issues at each new school and foster placement, although the state had continued to move him up each year because of his age and lack of evident mental retardation. He was a thirteen-year-old fourth grader.

All of this was revealing, but it was not what stunned me. The whole time Ms. Watson spoke, she kept the white sheet of paper tucked between her fingers, lifted a little as if to heighten my interest and stress its import. At the end, with an odd, conspiratorial delight on her face, she held out the paper. "You never saw this here, remember."

The paper was the report of the forensic psychologist assigned to the incident who had made Tevin a ward of the state. The psychologist, after a dozen interviews, had regressed the eight-year-old to a particular night at the apartment of a man named Dequarius Jones, who'd evidently been Tevin's mother's boyfriend. The boy had reluctantly entered the apartment, as he was scared of Mr. Jones. He'd called his mother's name, looked for her in the kitchen, the living room, and bedroom, and finally knocked on the bathroom door, where he could see from the bottom that the light was on. He knocked, called, waited and waited, and finally found the courage to open the door. There was his mother, lying prone in the tub. All down her shoulders and chest and all over the white porcelain was blood from her throat, which had been slit open from clavicle to clavicle. Tevin had run to her, had shaken her and shaken her, crying and screaming, had even tried to lift her from the tub and get her somehow to her feet, so that when the police finally found him hours later, he was soaked in his mother's blood.

I read the transcript over and over, imagining Tevin in the washroom covered in blood—just him now. Alone. And I wished I could go to the boy and lead him away to rooms free of such horror and sorrow.

The next week, Tevin was back. He walked through the door moments before the bell and sat, his face blank, his gray eyes wary, waiting to see what I'd do. I kept an eye on him and taught the morning's lessons. Tevin never lifted his pencil, just slouched in his seat. After a time, he began tapping the edge of the desk, less rhythmic than nervous, and I didn't ask him to stop. He began to whistle, a tuneless twittering, and I didn't say a word in the name of quiet. By the time the children headed to PE, he was visibly agitated. When Tarvis let out a shout, crying, "Tevin pinch my neck," I pulled Tevin to the back of the line without comment, and walked beside

Tevin the rest of the way. As I sent the children into the gym, I took Tevin's sleeve. "Come on."

He glanced at my fingers on his sleeve, smiled, and looked away, but he followed me back to the room, whistling so the notes echoed eerily through the empty hall. Back in the room, I straightened desks and wiped the board. It was a bright, humid morning, and though the air conditioning unit spat cool through the room, the sun through the windows bounced stars of light from the legs of desks and the glossy posters on the wall. Tevin leaned uneasily against the door watching me and whistling louder and louder, pounding a beat to the door. I let him be until he stopped making noise and just stood.

Finally he spoke, his voice so quiet I couldn't make out the words over the mutter of the air conditioning.

"What was that?"

"You ain't gone beat me," he said.

"No."

He smiled and said nothing. I held his gaze until he glanced away at the ceiling.

"You know, Tevin," I said gently, "It must be tough, being on your own. Moving all the time. Not having anyone to trust."

He was still staring at the ceiling.

I waited. In the hall, a class clattered past with a burst of echoing footfalls, leaving a deeper silence after they were gone.

Suddenly, Tevin slammed his hands to the door, making me jump. He didn't smile or look away, but spoke directly to me. "You don't know me." He opened the door and walked out, didn't look back as I ordered him to stop. Finally, I called the office to tell them Tevin Downs had just left my class—and I didn't know where he was headed.

That afternoon, as I went to sign out in the office, the secretary pointed to Mrs. Burtonsen's office. "She want to see you," she said. "'Bout that Downs boy."

I knocked at the heavy oak door, heard a stirring before the door was unlocked, and Mrs. Burtonsen was there with her generous smile, her gray hair pulled to tight curls with a fresh permanent.

"Mr. Copperman," she said. "How are you this afternoon?"

"Good, ma'am. Good as I can be."

"Well all right, then." She motioned for me to take a seat, went around the desk, and sat and leaned toward me. "This situation with Tevin Downs is troubling me," she said.

I nodded. "Did he leave the school grounds today?"

She brushed aside my question and kept speaking. "Mr. Winston cannot discipline the boy because he protects himself against punishment. Yet the boy clearly needs to be put in his place. His guardian tells me he cannot catch the boy to—punish him."

"Mr. Johnson told me the same thing. I saw about his mother, the streets of Midnight—"

"We are not really here to deal with his history, Mr. Copperman," Mrs. Burtonsen interjected. "That is beyond the bounds of what we can do. We are here to educate him. His guardian and his social worker, whom I spoke to today, both concur. The boy needs discipline. I have tried to speak to him, and as you've no doubt seen, he just turns his head and ignores you—he is deaf to reason. The question, then, becomes quite simple: is there a man who can teach the boy real respect? Or will he be—unfit—for school here at Promise-Upper, as he is thirteen years old, and by District guidelines ought properly to already be resourced and at the middle school?"

In the silence that followed, I saw what Mrs. Burtonsen

was asking: either I get the boy into shape somehow, through force of manhood or fist, or Promise-Upper would be done with him for good. Finally I cleared my throat. "Yes, ma'am, I suppose that's the question."

She took a deep breath, sighed, put a hand to my elbow across the desk. "All right then, Mr. Copperman. I just wanted to be sure you knew the situation. I'm glad we have an understanding."

We do not really, ma'am, I thought, as I shook her hand and fled the office.

The next day the air in the classroom was stale and still and warm—the air-conditioning unit had broken. By eight a.m., the classroom was sweltering, and sweat poured down my face, wet rings on the chest of each child's polo shirt, the scent of body thick through the room. Tevin's chair sat empty as I taught, and I couldn't pretend it wasn't a relief not to deal with him. I sweated out my undershirt. The sun through the windows made me squint so that I could hardly see the children, whose papers were spotted with drops of sweat. Around ten, the door opened and Tevin Downs walked in grinning. He was wearing the wrong color uniform, his polo red Friday when it was only Wednesday.

"Hi, Tevin. Have a seat," I said.

He walked to the front of the room until he stood inches from me. He wasn't sweating, seemed cool and calm.

"Sit down," I repeated. "Now."

He met my eyes and stepped closer still, until his face was inches from mine, and spoke, his breath hot to my cheek. "No."

"Sit!"

"You can't make me do nothing."

"You will sit down now."

He hocked, a throaty sound, and then, as the children gasped, he spit on my face. Some of it was in my eye, the wet, warm mucous sliding down my cheek, and anger and instinct rose in me. I seized him by the collar, rage summoning the strength of the college wrestler I'd been, and half lifted him off his feet, kicking and fighting, to the door of the classroom, throwing it open. "Get—out—of my classroom," I said, and tossed him in a great arc into the hall.

He tumbled to the floor as the children gasped. It felt—good. I wiped the spittle from my face with a sleeve as the children gaped. Tevin sat up, astonished, slowly brushed his shirt clean as I stood over him in the doorway. I waited for him to rise and come at me, for a sign of resentment, but instead he stood timidly, waited for me to move from the door to pass, shuffled quickly to his desk, and then, cheek to the desk, began the math worksheet he'd missed earlier in the morning. I looked about the room, and every child whose eyes had been on me turned down to the work there—for the moment, they were scared of me as I was scared now of myself.

As we sweated through the day, I saw in Tevin's subdued manner that his respect was authentic. I'd established dominance, the only order Tevin had ever known. And I felt ill with the knowledge that at the day's end, I'd tell Mrs. Burtonsen to resource the boy, to send him away—what he required, I couldn't afford to give.

PERSISTENCE AND PENANCE

And so went the minutes, hours, days, weeks, months, the rhythm of a young teacher's devotion: the rise at six a.m. and the first black pot of coffee, which I poured over two trays of ice and chugged in great forced gulps, half before the shower and half after; the quick steaming run of the iron over dress pants and dress shirt; and the ammoniac smell of the starch in a half-dark house. Then I was off into the morning heavy with promise, over Main and then Felicity in the car, the still distant world, people in motion beyond the windshield and, within, "Rosa Parks" by Outkast blaring loud—everybody move to the back of the bus and me trying to catch some rhythm and energy—and finally the school, still dark, mine the first car in the lot, and then the lights in the dark hallway, the rising crackle of filament and the skipping echo of my footsteps and finally the children waiting at the door, sleep-bleary faces turning toward me. Then, inside, the first voices, questions, tasks: children handing out morning math sheets, sweeping, settling themselves to reading as I wrote the daily math and language schedule on the chalkboard, the scratch and squeal and clamor of preparation, the clock ticking out the minutes until eight as the sun bloomed orange and filled the windows, everything subsumed in the task at hand, to this day and what it would exact in responsibility and necessity. The children were unaware and unwilling, would not thank me, would in fact curse me and play behind my back, but finally they trusted in their teacher, and so I did everything I could.

A forty-five-second bathroom break at nine-thirty on a normal Wednesday morning. Three boys on a clock, walking to a bathroom two doors down the hall while I watched from the doorway.

"I can go too, Mr. Copperman?" asked Charleton, standing even though it wasn't his turn.

"Don't speak out."

I glanced at the boys. Irvin was trouble, but had been good this morning. Tarvis was a hyper, sixty-pound bundle of craziness, but was sweet. Demetrius was bookish and quiet, had round, owlish glasses that the children teased him about, but was no problem—he seemed to want only to be left alone.

"Go too," I said to Charleton, and hit my stopwatch with an audible beep. I stood in the doorway and watched them go, four little uniformed backs retreating down the hall, piston arms pumping with hurry. There was a noise in the classroom, and I turned to see Tyreke hitting Talika.

"Pull a card," I said, pointing to his behavior chart on the wall, and counted out time with my hand. Tyreke's eyes went hard, and he knocked the papers from his desk, finally stood and pulled his card and slumped back to his seat. I glanced at the timer. Thirty-five seconds. I was proud of myself—a behavior problem dealt with, the rest of the class reading, and a bathroom break happening all at once. Then I heard an adult voice from the hall.

"Mr. Copperman, these boys were kicking this child in the bathroom in the dark," said Mrs. Barton, the special ed teacher whose classroom was just across from the bathroom. She stood now at the bathroom door.

"In the dark?"

"Somebody had turned the lights off," she said.

"And they were playing?" I asked, imagining Charleton roughhousing.

"Come on over and have a look," she said, crooking a finger. Reluctantly, I left the door to my room, aware that I would return to chaos. Standing with their backs to the tile wall were Charleton, Irvin, and Tarvis, breathing hard and looking sullen and guilty. Demetrius lay in a ball on the floor, one arm protecting his head, the other shielding his stomach.

"They were all three kicking that boy," said Mrs. Williams.

"All three?" I repeated. I looked at Tarvis, who wouldn't meet my eyes.

"All three," she said, and walked away. I glared at the boys, then bent over Demetrius, who sat as I knelt beside him.

"Are you OK?"

His eyes focused as he felt along the tile, found his glasses, and slid them back on. They were crooked, and I gently straightened them. He looked at me, then up at the boys, and nodded. I gave him another few seconds, then took his hand and pulled him to his feet.

When I turned to the boys, I couldn't speak, just pointed silently to the door. Back in the room, half the class was standing and talking. I didn't bother quieting or reprimanding them, just sat at my desk as the clamor persisted and began writing office referrals, unable to care if they got licks. There was nothing else to do.

Sometimes the Delta shocked and stunned—where was the justice for these children? I struggled to recognize that not only couldn't I create new lives for my kids, but on my worst days I couldn't even make progress in teaching them to read, write, and understand fractions. For a time, I approached each day with resignation, entered the classroom with a flinch. Many of these children had hard lives, and they brought their circumstances to school with them. Some were filled with so much need and hurt and anger they filled the air with the intensity of their pain, howled out and pointed fingers, tattled mercilessly, called each other the cruelest names they could, ganged up on the weakest in the dark. How can one respond to constant disrespect without anger? I tried and tried to remain calm. Every day I told myself I'd remain patient, speak quietly and softly, but by eleven thirty I'd become a violent and petty dictator, hauling students off by their shirt collars and slamming my palm to desktops and yelling to be heard over the din. I wanted so badly to help, and they wouldn't even let me be kind to them.

One morning I grew so angry at the children for not standing in a quiet line that I forced the entire class out into a winter downpour, insisting we would stand until we could be silent. We all stood there in the hard, cold rain, them screaming at each other to be quiet and then screaming at me until finally I brought them back inside. I stood at the front of the classroom, dripping wet, facing everyone I'd soaked, and the shame at what I'd done and who I'd become filled me as I took in their wet, unhappy faces. In a war of wills, they had outlasted me. We stared at each other, and after a time I apologized, and then we sat in a longer and still sullen silence. It was early in the day and there were things I'd planned to teach, but I'd lost the authority to ask anything.

Monthly, Teach For America brought Delta corps members together regionally or all at once for a so-called All-Corps. These gatherings featured workshops, troubleshooting sessions, check-ins, presentations, and motivational speakers. The sessions, which always took place on a Saturday, inevitably involved a drive, given the vast spread of corps members; some corps members in Quitman County would drive a hundred and fifty miles to make a nine a.m. start time. Even when the All-Corps was closer—perhaps only forty minutes away from those of us in Promise to go to the most common location, an auditorium and classrooms on the Delta State Campus in Cleveland, Mississippi—it was hard to wake early after a long week to make the trip. There was rejuvenating energy in the sessions, a temporary return to the feel of the institute, where thousands of us all together, committed to the "mission," had given those five weeks a feel of political rally and rock concert. And, too, afterward, there was the chance for social contact, which many of us were starved for—we'd been accustomed to college, to being surrounded by peers our own age with similar backgrounds, while in the Delta there were often only three or four corps members in a given town or school, and some corps members lived on farms or in trailers far from neighbors.

The problem with these Saturday sessions, however, was the ways it was possible to measure oneself against others and despair. Second-year corps members ran most of the workshops, usually featuring examples of curricula or best practices from their classrooms that they felt were particularly effective. We were presented with example after example, and the necessity of measurable success was constantly hammered home: whatever we did in the classroom, we had to prove our results in actionable numbers. Second-years would teach a mini-lesson, a perfectly crafted little jewel of benchmark applied, and present colorful graphs with percentages of perfect proficiency—in their classrooms, it seemed that every student met the standards of excellence. These were the early days of No Child Left Behind, when the policy seemed in line with Teach For America's mission to offer every child equal educational opportunity, and so we were told that to teach well was to generate testable, demonstrable outcomes, to lift our children to the land of relative quantitative perfection. The distance between the immaculate graphs of the second-years and the strident voices of my children questioning my authority was hard to reconcile; often, I found myself feeling more hopeless than inspired.

The Saturday of the first All-Corps my first year, I was exhausted—the week had gone terribly, and I didn't have any idea how to teach; I would have settled for guidance in how to stop yelling. At nine a.m., a pot of coffee consumed on the drive to Delta State, I hurried through the humid parking lot and found a seat in the back of the first session, a stern look shot my way from the program director for being late: the culture of Teach For America prescribed that you be on time and exhibit a good attitude. I can only imagine how surly a look I must have shot back, for later that day I found myself being pulled aside by my manager, who asked searchingly whether things were going all right, noting that I seemed a little "out of sorts." I grinned, joked, affected the unassailable sincerity I've always deployed for dealing with authority, and convinced my manager that all was fine. What strikes me now is how steadfastly I refused to admit to anyone, not just other corps members and my manager but even to friends and family, just how bad things were in my classroom. I didn't tell anyone that my goal each day wasn't significant achievement or to change a child's future, but to make it to three-fifteen without a fight breaking out. To admit the truth seemed to betray the possibility that things could be different. Instead, I kept my mouth shut and took notes regarding all the effective practices of the second-year corps members, and hoped that I could pretend to be teaching until I figured out how.

Only slowly did I begin to understand how divided a society I'd entered. I'd always noticed the absence of any white people at all on the black side of town, how the other Teach For America teachers were stared at outside school, though for a time I found it hard to distinguish their particular treatment because of the way I was stared at by everyone on both sides of town. Most restaurants my fellow corps members and I frequented were "nicer" ones with mostly white patrons—there was a café with a Delta-wide reputation in a brick building at the edge of the mostly empty downtown that did a lovely oven-baked catfish in a tureen with butter and herbs and light biscuits and crumpets fresh and smothered in jam and clotted cream. The group of us who regularly met there Sunday mornings stood out for being younger and for our accents, and certainly I was always the only Asian person present, the diners white and the serving staff black except for the hostess and owner, who moved about the tables welcoming and greeting. I did a tour one evening of the country club, which had a small golf course and a restaurant and tennis court and gym, but walking through I saw Talika's mother there in a server's whites, and the doorman and handyman and groundskeeper and bartender all were also black and wore servers' button-up uniforms, and I realized that here, the old ways were preserved; when I walked into the weight room, several silver-haired old men stopped their conversations and lifting to stare with a mix of curiosity and hostility, and I realized that even if I paid the fee I couldn't ever really "join." In Promise, blacks and whites mixed at businesses like Walmart and at banks and gas stations and corporate chains like Waffle House, but socially they remained worlds apart.

When we did a writing assignment about nightmares, Talika's dream was: "I sawed a mean white man with a knife, and he come in the night and stab me and my family and blood is everywhere and I scream but no one does nothing to help."

I questioned her about the caption and the nightmare.

"Talika, do you actually know any white people?" I asked.

"Naw, Mr. Copperman," she said. "You the first not-black person I ever talked to in my life. It just that I know how white people do!"

I looked at her paper, where she'd drawn a fanged ghoul, features blurred by overapplication of white crayon; all about lay figures with *x*'s for eyes and open mouths, while over everything were great strokes of red crayon for blood. "Not all white people," I said. "My own father is white, you know."

"Your papa WHITE?" she said incredulously. Then she nodded her head as if she'd figured out an exemption for my questionable origins. "It OK, Mr. Copperman," she said. "He ain't from around *here*."

I tried to think of what to say but could come up with no adequate response. Lynching in adjacent counties was in the memory of her parents and grandparents; who was I to claim that change had come in a place so substantially unaltered by time? Here at this school, even now, we kept black children fenced in with barbed wire, and at the Academy football field I passed on my way home each day, hoops of razor wire kept them out.

One day I called the janitor, Deborah Burns, to my classroom door, where I had Tarvis, her nephew, firmly by the shirt-sleeve.

"This boy," I said, "needs to explain his behavior to you."

I was angry and frustrated. Tarvis hadn't done work in days, had taken to throwing things, making animal noises and talking back constantly.

"Hold it," said Deborah, raising a palm. She was usually relaxed, deliberate, and slow moving, but now she looked at me with her mouth set hard and tight.

"*This boy* has a name," she said. "His name is Tarvis."

I looked down at all seventy pounds of Tarvis, his eyes

narrowed with fury, little hands clenched into fists. I'd called him—boy? Erased his name? What need did I have to make a four-foot fourth grader feel smaller? What was wrong with me? I apologized to Deborah, who laid Tarvis out but good for his behavior, but I couldn't recover my righteous anger. What was this work doing to me, that I was losing dignity and principles? What was I becoming?

One refuge I found was a Chinese restaurant off the highway called the China-King Buffet. The unlit, hand-painted sign was all that distinguished the plain, square, white building from the industrial uses of the row of identical buildings beside it; the windows out front were covered, and the first time I went I was a little scared of what I'd find inside. The space was vast, high ceilinged, and unpartitioned, so that the modest buffet that steamed constant clouds from the egg-flower soup tank looked comically small, and the old Formica tables and cheap folding chairs seemed unreasonably distant from one another, each table its own solitary island even on nights when the tables were full, which usually they were not. There was a sense that it was a small operation striving to fill an overlarge space, an impression heightened by the attempt to fill the long walls with pictures of properly large scale: the entire rear wall was a twenty-foot by hundred-foot color picture of the Great Wall of China receding into blue sky, splitting the restaurant in two down the middle, while on each adjoining wall hand-painted gold koi of monstrous proportions undulated across the otherwise empty space. One of the oddest features of the place was how on weekend nights it was often divided by race, with blacks on the left, on one side of the Great Wall, and whites on the other side; fittingly, I often ended up in the middle, directly beneath the Great Wall. In the furthest corner from the entrance was a desk and cash register and a single open door, which was bright with the lights of the kitchen behind; every time I entered, a short, slight Chinese boy of fifteen or sixteen was perched on a stool beside the desk with a Chinese-language magazine or book in hand, and he would startle at the clang of the bells on the door and thrust the magazine under the desk and leap forward with a stack of menus, speaking broken, heavily accented English: "Welcome. Help to the buffet if y'all like, please!"

The first time I went in, I looked over the buffet and knew it was for a Delta palate—everything was fried and thoroughly inauthentic for the Szechuan cuisine the menu claimed, shrimp and chicken and noodles and battered vegetables. When I called the boy over and asked to order off the menu, he brightened and nodded and said, "Oh yes, you are Asian!" When the steamed dumplings and buns came, the platter was brought out by a small, kind-faced woman in an apron whom I took to be the boy's mother, and when she saw me her face lit up, and she slid the steaming food in front of me and put her hand to my shoulder and motioned for the boy to come translate; through his translation, she indicated welcome for "another Asian person!" She tried to hide her disappointment at my questionably Japanese origins and said several times just how welcome I was; finally, she retreated to the kitchen and let me eat, and I was delighted to find the food good, fresh, and flavorful—and not fried. When I finished, the boy brought with the check a giant plate of dessert from the buffet, lime Jello with whipped cream and white cake and pudding, which he indicated was on the house and which I tried to move around on the plate so as to appear to have enjoyed it. And so the pattern became set—whether I came with a group of other TFA teachers or alone, there was always a complimentary plate of dessert, and always a warm reception, the only place in the town where I was not the only slant-eyed, brown-skinned fellow.

Over time, in conversations with the boy, Hao, on quiet days, I found out a little more: the family had come over not long ago to a restaurant in New Jersey, and when relatives who'd run this restaurant decided to leave they'd agreed to come take over, with no idea about what being Chinese immigrants might mean in the deep rural South. Hao went to the public schools, to the high school; he told me, in his broken English with his overpronounced syllables and troubled *l*'s and *r*'s, that he had no friends, that he wanted to return to Jersey or to China, that America was not as he'd thought it would be. I couldn't imagine how difficult it was for him at the high school—I knew from my experience of the streets the pointed fingers and the laughter, the taunts of *Chinaman, Chinaman, show us some Kung Fu!*

One day when I came on a quiet afternoon Hao's face lit up when I entered. He called out "Hey! I got something for you!" and gestured for me to find a seat; then he hurried back to the kitchen. Moments later, the music, which had been new country, went silent, and then there was a crackle and first quiet and then, at earsplitting volume, the first notes of a flute, and for a moment I didn't recognize it and then I did: a vintage recording of "Sakura," the cherry blossom song, that most common Japanese folksong so often used when teaching about Japan. I nearly burst into laughter, then restrained myself. Who knew where Hao had found the CD here, in a town without a record store—it certainly must have taken some effort.

Hao walked out of the back with a proud grin, the flute notes echoing loud from wall to wall, and called over the clamor, "I got this for you. Do you like it?"

I told him I loved it, that it was everything I missed, and

he nodded and nodded, beaming, imagining he'd returned home to me in a way that he himself must have longed for so acutely—a reminder of who he was, where he'd come from, that made him feel for a moment he had a place in the world.

One day, Talika put this poem in my mailbox:

A Poem to Mr. Copperman

Kid's in your room need to
Show you respect
Includeing me. One day I will show you respect
And they will too. I know you got your education and you
Is trying to help us get ours

But you just want do right.
Thank you mr. Copperman
I will do Better some day!!!

Love,
Talika

Below the poem was a picture rendered in pencil and colored with highlighter that showed a group of boys and girls joining hands in a line. They were all wide eyed and smiling; each figure bore the name of a student in our class. I stood in the middle of the circle, my curly hair a mushroom cloud of ringlets, my legs half as big again as my torso, my stick arms outstretched as if to embrace every student all at once.

Perhaps hope remained in persistence alone—for each morning, the children were there again in the dim hall, backs leaning into the door, waiting for my arrival. The day before might have been awful—I may have yelled, broken chalk in frustration, put my fist to the wall as I did one day when I couldn't get even a moment of attention. But the children returned, they forgave, they arrived again at my door waiting for me to teach them, to make good on the only promise I could keep—to stand at the front of the classroom and try. And so each day I began anew.

Since the age of four, I'd trained in the martial art of aikido in the style of Shin Shin Toitsu, a particularly philosophical branch of the art. Aikido is exclusively a defensive art, based primarily on the principle of "nondescension"; it aims to teach harmony and peace, to navigate conflict without engaging in a "fight." My father is a fifth-degree black belt and has his own dojo in Eugene, Oregon, where I began training; my mother is a second-degree black belt. By the age of seventeen, I had my own *shodan*, or black belt, and at Stanford I convinced my wrestling coach to let me teach a class to friends and other interested parties during the spring off-season. I enjoyed teaching, felt comfort in having my feet on the mat and the familiar routines and exercises and *waza*, or throws and series of throws, that filled my childhood. I went to Principal Burtonsen and proposed an after-school aikido class.

"But how will y'all do that karate on the floor?" she asked skeptically.

I called my father, who convinced the Northwest Ki Federation and the Oregon Ki Society to buy gymnastics mats and send them out. I asked for "enough" to accommodate a dozen students. One day, I received a call over the intercom, informing me that an aide was coming to take my class so I could go deal with the "truck." I found the gray-haired gym teacher, Mr. Holiday, and Mrs. Burtonsen standing out in the sun with a semitrailer and a pale, tall white truck driver wearing a tank top and cowboy hat who looked uncomfortable standing stuck in the sun with black people. When he saw me, he shook his head and said, "Huh," as if my presence both baffled and explained everything. "You the one who can sign for these all?" he said.

I nodded, signed. The driver opened the rear of the truck, pulled down the ramp, and gestured for me to go in. "All yours," he said.

Mrs. Burtonsen and Mr. Holiday and I blinked into the dark, and then Mr. Holiday, from whom I'd always felt a low-level resentment as though my being another male at the elementary school somehow made me competition, began to chuckle. "My God, Mr. Copperman," he said. "You starting up a karate academy?"

The gymnastics mats were new, each folding panel encased in clear plastic. Even in the dim interior the red, blue, and yellow panels were bright, and looked new and expensive. They were stacked tight and high all the way to the front of the truck, a solid block of primary colors. Thirty panels, enough mats to cover one full half of a basketball court, more mat space than most professional dojos can boast. As I later found out, my father had insisted that it made no sense to invest halfway, had pitched me as a missionary of modern aikido moving through rich and unexplored territory. They had invested thousands of dollars in the mats, which took me thirty minutes to move and stack in the hot sun. Mrs. Burtonsen watched me for a time as I grunted and hauled, hurrying to get back to my class and a little embarrassed, a bemused smile on her lips at the disjunction between the old gym and the cinder-block buildings and this shiny new equipment. When she left me to finish, she put a hand to my shoulder and said, "Well, Mr. Copperman, we certainly can't wait to see what you can do with all *this*."

I put up fliers throughout the school, went to classrooms on my free period to advertise, got permission to pitch my class in an assembly. I heard children talking about it in the school, *Y'all heard 'bout that Chinaman gone teach that karate class?*, and smiled and didn't correct them about the name of the martial art or my cultural background. With trepidation, one Wednesday afternoon I finished teaching and sent the kids who usually lingered in the classroom home early, and took my gi bag to the boy's bathroom. I knew full well the appeal and authority of uniform, and the regalia of an aikido shodan is considerable: in addition to a thick cotton gi with long, wide sleeves embroidered with the patch of the Oregon Ki Society and the traditional Kanji *ki* symbol, and a black belt about the waist, instructors wear a *hakama*, a jet-black, intricately pleated kimono-style trouser secured with a complex series of knotted straps. I stepped out of the bathroom and into the hall, and every child and adult I passed stopped in stunned silence. The samurai arrives in the Delta at long last, I thought, as I approached the gym. Behind me, I heard the office door open, and the secretary and Mrs. Washburn, another teacher on my hall, hurried out—evidently someone had told them to have a look. I waved at them and pushed the gym doors open.

Inside were nearly thirty children, most of them boys. Their voices had been clamorous and still echoed, but most went silent as they saw me. One boy, late to notice, a fifth grader known for being difficult, had his back to me and was the last to stop talking. He turned, and his eyes went wide. "Ooowee!" he said with a mix of surprise and delight.

I'd had a late free period when the gym was empty and had

already laid out the mats. "Please remain silent, and make a straight line facing me," I said as I walked toward them. Jostling a little, they complied. One boy had his arms crossed, and I went to him and touched his elbow and said, "Arms at your sides," and all along the lines children thrust their arms down. A fifth-grade girl, who towered above all the rest of the children and who had a habit of slouching, stood before me, her head hunched down, as was her habit. "Please stand up straight," I said, raising my own head and straightening my lower back, and the line complied. I stood before them, bent down and removed my shoes, and then arranged them by my feet with each toe parallel. "Please remove your shoes and then return to line."

There was quick shuffle and patter as shoes came off; I walked the line, corrected one pair that wasn't straight and one pair that was out of line, and soon the shoes were in a straight line and the students stood just behind. The children's eyes were bright with excitement and intrigue, and I stood before them and felt, for the first time since I had been in the Delta, that perhaps I did know how to teach something after all.

I raised my hands to take in the bright squares of mat on the basketball court, the hoops and their sagging nets, the white halogens in their wire cages, and the overhead fan turning circles in the recesses of the vaulted ceiling.

"Welcome to our dojo," I said. "Here, you may call me Sensei."

I'd like to say that I finally enchanted my children and transformed my classroom as easily as I commanded the attention of my aikido students, but that wasn't what happened. Days weren't easy in November, a nightmare of frustration and chaos, or even in early January, when summer was impossibly distant. What changed was that I lost first Antiquarian and then Tevin, two of the boys who had been causing the worst problems. With them gone, though I still had a difficult set of kids, I began to gain control of the class. Children could actually listen to lessons, and they stopped arguing consequences and started doing their work. I was able to joke, to ease up and take them to recess without fear of what would happen, to loosen my tie and play a game of kickball on the grass field out back, or to stand and for a moment enjoy silence as the children stayed on task. Some days when everything went right and I stood at the front during readers' workshop and watched my students reading their books and writing in their journals, lips working silent syllables, a tongue in the corner of the mouth, the only sounds the tick of the wall clock and the occasional scratch of pencil to paper, and the light through the windows golden and bright, limning the edges of upheld pages and desktops and the profiles of downturned faces, I would try to memorize it, afraid that I might never have such a moment again. And then a hand would rise, and I'd go to answer a question or help a student find a new book, grateful to be needed.

In this newly functional classroom, students' actual academic needs began to be distinguishable from their behavior. Charleton was disinclined to do his reading at all, and I discovered that this was in fact because he was reading at only a second-grade level, yet when he applied himself he was perhaps the best math student. Much of his acting out during math was due in fact to boredom: he'd already finished his work. I set aside extra time during readers' workshop, and set an extra packet of advanced work in math on his desk, each finished packet redeemable for a bag of hot chips (and me not at all now above a little bribery), and suddenly he was less of a problem. Tarvis, on the other hand, was often confused in math—it turned out he'd either missed the day I taught multiplication or failed to understand what we were trying to do, but though he'd tried to memorize the times tables he didn't actually know what the multiplication sign meant. One computer period with me at the board, and I was able to show him, at which point he said, with a mix of pride and surprise, "Man, shoot, that's *easy!*"

Talika loved to read, and when I kept her after school or convinced her to focus, she would giggle aloud with delight as she read the A to Z mysteries that she found particularly funny. When introduced to the "Captain Underpants" books, she couldn't believe the author was allowed to write such jokes. "Isn't books supposed to be all *serious* and *important?*" she asked after school one day, brandishing the book in one hand for emphasis. She'd just laughed her way through the flip section, exclaiming aloud with delight. "Cause this is just *funny!*"

"If it's not serious enough for you, there's the Mississippi history textbook there for you to read," I said.

She glanced at the thick textbook, which she and the rest of the children uniformly hated, and clutched the book to her chest and returned to the corner, me grinning at her retreat.

One boy, Nyson, I finally started to notice. He was moon faced and dull eyed and never closed his mouth all the way, his slug of tongue perpetually protruding. He arrived early to my classroom and lingered in a wistful, patient manner that begged response. He did not know what he wanted, that much was clear from the way he wandered the bookshelves for the four-thousandth time. Often, he stood beneath the "Holler at Our Scholars!" work board eyeing his perfect tens tables, the only assignment he'd done well enough for me to justify putting up. It was ridiculous to celebrate the tens table; if you could count to ten, you could multiply your way through by adding zeros after the digit. Nyson hadn't actually shown mastery—he'd scored ten out of eleven but demonstrated no understanding of what he was doing. When he reached ten, the double-digit number had thrown him, and he'd concluded that ten sets of ten was ten and written 010, unsure which side to favor. I'd decided to celebrate the small victory: he'd nearly passed, which was closer than he'd come on any other assignment. On the Scantron math diagnostic I started the year with, he'd somehow managed to miss every problem, had even marked *D*, none of the above, for several answers. *D* had not been an option on the test. He'd scored a true zero.

What was worst was the way he'd return again and again to gaze at the scholar board, slack jawed, eyeing the smiley face I'd drawn on his test with my red pen, the "10/11! Great Job, Nyson!" scrawled at the top. If I paused behind him, he'd point with a rapturous finger, grin with white teeth, his slack tongue retreating for a moment, and I'd return the smile, clap him on the back, and murmur something encouraging, to which he always replied quietly, "Yes, sir, Mr. Copperman." I was not encouraged by his other work. This was Nyson's first time through fourth grade, but he'd already failed third grade. Mrs. Burtonsen indicated that if I failed him, he'd eventually be resourced to an age-appropriate special education classroom according to Mississippi policy: "Two times through two grades has got to be enough," she said when I asked. According to Nyson's file, despite minimal test scores each year he'd never been tested for learning disability or IQ—the children who were tested in Promise were the problem kids, the bad boys who presented behavioral challenges. Nyson was too polite and quiet to present a problem, so he'd been judged not to have one. When I requested testing, Mrs. Burtonsen had frowned, leaned back in her desk. "See what you can do with him in your classroom, Mr. Copperman," she said. "If he had an issue, it would have been caught the last time he failed. Go on and take care of the rest of your children."

I refused Mrs. Burtonsen's mandate to wait and let the inevitable take its course—or at least, I'd no intention of accepting it. I called on Nyson whenever I could, gave him the attention I could spare, and encouraged his negligible progress. I had all I could handle each day with so many children, their unending demands rendered in antics, shouts, actionable successes, and failures. Nyson lingered at the margin, transfixed by his achievement, waiting for me to recognize it again and again, to confirm that he'd done well. It pained me, and despite better intentions I sometimes skirted him in the morning or afternoon if I saw him near the board, a devotive figure at the altar of his inadequate success.

Talika Johnson, never one to allow vulnerability to go unremarked, would mock him if I didn't watch her closely: she'd stand behind him as he looked, let her face go slack, tongue lolling from her mouth and eyes large with affected wonder. The first time, I took her by the elbow, steered her away, and whispered an emphatic, "Don't."

She snorted. "Why? He don't notice."

I told Talika to stop being unkind, that it was unnecessary. Nyson did know the difference—he avoided Talika, and more than once I'd seen him retreat to the back of the lunch line or leave a prime reading spot when she neared. Yet privately I agreed: Nyson was an unpleasant feature of the landscape, a net loss, a zero.

One cool winter morning Nyson and Talika arrived early, and Talika immediately began filing graded papers. It was a Friday and it had been a long week of labor and bad behavior, the days lightless and slow, the grind of ritual unrelieved. The heater groaned and rattled through the cold room, gave an insufficient heat. Nyson wandered to his place by the board, and I started to go to him but stopped—the idea of congratulating him yet again seemed unendurable. Talika was watching me, met my eye and grinned at my flinch. I looked away. "I'm going to the restroom," I said, and stepped into the hall, the bulbs sputtering as they warmed. In the echoic boy's room, the water was cold as I washed my hands. I was two steps from the classroom door when I heard the shriek, an animal fury, and ran in.

Talika held Nyson's test over her head and appeared poised to rip it in two. Nyson was a different child, his hands clenched in fists, jaw tight and eyes huge with desperation.

"What's going on here?" I demanded. Nyson snatched for the paper, missed, and screamed again. Talika backed away.

"Ten of eleven ain't no passing grade for no times table," Talika said, circling from Nyson with the paper raised. "He get all crazy-angry, and I think he's gone hit me, so I grab this up to keep him off. And he start hollering like that."

"Nyson," I said, lowering my voice. "It's fine. She'll put down the paper."

He glanced at me and shook his head. "No," he said, his voice loud and clear—present like I'd never heard it. His eyes met mine. "It true I ain't did nothing right?"

"No, now, you did well," I said soothingly, stepping toward him.

He lunged toward Talika and got a grip on the test. The sound was audible. He groaned, lifted the torn paper in a shaking hand, tears rolling down his cheek.

Talika hid behind me. "I didn't mean to," she said.

"Nyson, look," I said. I took the other half of the test from Talika and held it out to him. "We'll put it back together."

He took the halves, face convulsing with grief. "It can't be like it were," he choked. He wiped his nose with a sleeve, looked at me with judging eyes. "You a liar, Mr. Copperman." He offered the two halves of the test. When I didn't take them, his eyes flashed. "Take it!"

I took it.

He examined the room with disgust, turned, and left, footsteps retreating down the hall. Talika and I went to the door and watched him walk the long hall. He did not look back.

Nyson returned the next day, unchanged except now there was no test gazing. It made him easier to ignore, which filled me with guilt whenever I looked at the empty space on the scholar board. I kept the test, even taped it back together, but when I asked him if he wanted it back up he looked away and refused to speak, and I never asked again. At first I made an effort with him, stopped by his desk with every assignment, but soon enough he blended in—there was a classroom of children clamoring for my attention in louder, brighter ways. The year passed, a series of crises avoided or weathered, Nyson failing everything, hovering on the margins unnoticed. When it came time to give grades, he was the only student I couldn't find a way to pass, and I told myself it was just—Nyson simply hadn't done the work. I felt a small, sick shock—despite other intentions, I had actually done exactly as Mrs. Burtonsen had suggested. Surely it wasn't my fault—it was Nyson himself. Everything about the boy disappeared.

The next school year, I was surprised to find that he hadn't yet been resourced: he was placed in another Teach For America corps member's classroom for another run through fourth grade, and he seemed to do better there than he had in my class—sometimes I saw him, down the hall, smiling when she praised him, and sometimes I watched him out on the recess field playing kickball and turning flip after flip. I told myself that there was nothing more I could have done. Near the end of the next year, I asked his teacher how he'd done. "Well, he's being automatically resourced given his age and history of failure," she said. "I couldn't do much with him, even though he's eager to please. Next week, they're testing him for SPED," meaning special education. I shook my head at the idea that now, two years later, they would give him learning tests—evidently testing had to occur before a child could be put in resource, even in a process initiated by age.

When the paperwork appeared in my box, it included a photocopy from the teacher who now taught Nyson with a sticky note saying, "Thought you'd want to know." I didn't want to read on but forced myself to look. Then, when I'd read it three times, I pawed through the files in my desk, found last year's test scores and other papers I'd kept, and rifled through them until I unearthed the test, held the original proof of my inadequacy: 10 times 10 is 010.

The psychometrist had determined that Nyson was of normal IQ but suffered from severe dyslexia and dyscalculia, getting his words and numbers disordered. They were resourcing him anyway: he was now too old for his grade, whatever his disability. The diagnosis was too late.

I'd failed Nyson, had missed the meaning of his first zero on the diagnostic and every subsequent sign, even his own writing on the wall. All those months he begged me to notice, and I let him suffer there alone, the only one who cared enough to look in the right place.

I would like to lie and say I fought the process, tried to make amends, but I didn't protest. In truth, it wouldn't have made a difference.

My penance is that now I must remember him as he actually was: begging to be noticed as I wished him gone, until he actually disappeared.

CLUB SWEET

Of that first year in the Delta, much is gone, and what remains are moments and images that are brief and overperfect, which is how time textures the past, sharpens memory to metaphor. A defiant, proud little girl atop a desk, declaiming with outstretched arms. A boy's hand on a doorframe. Dust motes in a beam of light cast in a dim hall as a boy turns backflip after backflip. A kickball game on the grass field, a scent of fresh-mowed grass and dust and heat, a beckoning boy calling, "Pitch it, Mr. C," and a ball booted skyward in a comet's arc over the fence and the street and even the house next door as we all stand and gape. The silence of a classroom of children reading on some high bright afternoon with a sun pouring gold through the windows, a rare moment when all eyes inclined down and all lips mouthed the read words while I stood there in the center of the room, beaming.

I lived with a terrible isolation. Sometimes, I'd drive to a weekend party one or two hundred miles away, or travel up Highway 61 to Memphis and the comfort of a coffee shop in Midtown, an Indian restaurant, a night at a bar. But my life in Promise consisted mostly of the classroom. Evenings I drove to the highway strip and parked behind the mall with its empty lot and dirty blank windows, abandoned except for a lonely army recruiting office that no one ever seemed to enter or leave, though the sign in the window was always lit. I'd keep the engine on for the air conditioning and watch cars pass on the highway, tailing clouds of dust, one after another, in a furious hurry to get from one flat, hot end of town to the other. I'd watch people leaving the safety of their vehicles to pump their gas or buy beer and smokes at the

Double-Quick, proceeding ponderously, each step and action a deliberate, drowsy effort through the thick hot air. I liked to imagine them having come from their separate lives—the white man with coarse thinning gray hair come straight from the catfish ponds, mud-caked boots with the mud lightening as it dried, the young black man fresh escaped from school, walking a dip and sway in his uniform already altered at first escape: the khakis below the hips and sinking, the navy shirt twisted into a turban, dark arms and shoulders exposed by a yellowed wife-beater tucked into plaid boxers.

I'd run after dark when it cooled. The hot wet air and filmy dark would close about me, and everything would become the rasp of breath and the beat of feet on the pavement. The sidewalk was gray in the darkness, the cracks' hazy lines passing beneath, cockroaches scrambling from my feet in brown blurs, fleeing for gutters and grass. I'd come to Magnolia Avenue, turn toward downtown. The broad, columned porches and shuttered windows of colonials would fall away as I found my stride. Small flying insects would bat my face, clouds of them spinning gold cones in the streetlights, and underfoot the streets would melt and pass. Sometimes, the sudden roar of an air-conditioning unit or the howl of a dog, the distant rush of highway like the ocean loud in a shell—there but not there, and then the play of headlights through a gap between buildings, the roar of a pickup grinding gears, the rake of eyes from an open window, sometimes hoots, hollers, sometimes a man calling unintelligibly, and I'd keep my eyes to the road, just running, and most times they'd pass without incident.

Once, a great black pickup with monster-truck wheels passed in the opposite lane, and then with a scream of brakes cut a three-point in the road and loomed behind, too big for the lane, rising behind me with tires off the road as I jumped into the roadside culvert that drained to the bayou, felt the side mirror pass an inch off my shoulder and heard howls of excitement, twanged cords of a country song, and landed in the mud, warm dark water to my knees, the engine roaring and roaring as the taillights receded.

I stayed off that street after that, found my route, streets with flag-draped colonials set back from the road and the life within contained, seen from lit windows, and the dogs fenced back in a garden, and if I was noticed it was by the ghost of a face peering through window glass at a hundred paces, and me surely grown familiar after a time, expected during the evening meal or the dishes afterward, part of the routine of these lives I had no knowledge of but moved through nightly.

One afternoon near the end of the school year Mrs. Mason stopped by after school and told me I should come out with her and a few "friends" for a drink on Friday—"folks you know," she said, which when I pressed her turned out to mean a thirtyish fifth-grade teacher, Mrs. Hudson, a third-grade aide, Ms. Beadle, and couple other teachers from Delta Horizon, a Title 1 after-school program. I knew Mrs. Hudson only in passing: She was a thick-bodied, big-bosomed woman with a shrill, screaming laugh that made you turn and look for its owner with the conviction she might be in pain. She seemed, too, to have a way with her students. Once, going to an assembly, my class had been lined up behind hers, and her lines were so straight and still it seemed she'd hypnotized each child and placed each a precise twelve inches behind the one in front; my students, with their restless, shuffling sway and loll, looked sloppy and ill managed, though they were on their best behavior. I knew Ms. Beadle better, had chatted with her a few times. She was in her early twenties, was quick to smile and spoke quietly with a rapid, uneven cadence, so that you were always straining to hear her and still felt you were missing something. She also wore too much eye makeup and lipstick, with clothes that were rather tight and revealing by Promise teacher standards. More than once, I'd noticed the older veterans eyeing her with the sly, smirking disapproval of the older woman, and had felt kinship—I'd felt the sting of their judgment as well.

"Where?" I asked.

"Club Sweet is all there is," she said, smiling. "Somebody would think you weren't from around here."

I smiled, feeling a twitch of recognition at the name "Sweet." Club Sweet was on this side of town on Felicity, just over the tracks—the only bar I knew in the county, and a genuine juke joint. It was low and long and roofed with tin, like most buildings on the black side of town. All that distinguished it was the plywood facade, which had "Club Sweet" painted across it in fading green. I passed it each morning on my way to school, the small dirt and gravel lot often littered with remains of the previous night's revelry. Sometimes there would be a few men standing around in front blinking into the dawn as if someone had flicked on lights in the middle of a movie theater. Coming home late on Fridays, my headlights cut a swath and caught the shining whites of eyes as someone went in or came out—there were rarely crowds out in front, but I had a sense of steady motion, proof that within was some liquored pulse. I'd been afraid to go alone—but here was a way in.

"I'll see you there," I said.

At five that Friday it was still warm, though the edge of the heat was cooling. The sun was coming down from its afternoon height and threw long, sharp shadows as I stepped to the school parking lot. I'd waited for everyone to leave, so it was on me to put the chains to the gate. There was no one to see the casual wear I'd worried endlessly over the night before. I'd donned the dark jeans, green-striped polo shirt, and tricolor Puma sneakers in the hand-streaked mirror of the boy's bathroom, added a new caking of deodorant and a fresh slick of hair product that did nothing to contain my curl. It was hopeless anyway: I'd be stared at in Club Sweet whatever I did. Given the inevitability of being a spectacle, I was at least a well-groomed one.

In the parking lot there were few cars, mostly run-down Chevy and Ford sedans, so Mrs. Mason's new red Hyundai Accent was prominent. I parked beside her Hyundai and got out, locked the door with an audible beep, and stood in the lot. On the street, I heard a child's voice. An older boy, square bodied and strutting, was walking with his arm about a tall, older-looking girl from Mrs. Mason's class who always struck me for her premature coquettishness—she had a preening, self-satisfied air, stood with her weight always on a heel, hip cocked and hands behind her back as if presenting herself for imminent adulation. The boy met my gaze and looked as if he was going to shout something, but the girl touched a hand to his elbow, and they kept on down Felicity. I was relieved—no trouble—and started across the gravel. There was nobody in front, no immediate signal of what lay within—just the wide wooden door on the green wall, paint scoured to reveal weather-grayed board beneath. I took a deep breath and opened the door.

Inside, the bare overhead bulbs were harsh, so everything took on a gray-green cast like film negatives on a black screen. Insects buzzed about the bulbs in unending circles. The floor was concrete—not a lacquered surface like a city club's but bare rock marked with the stains of spill and riot. The walls were covered in yellowed, tacked-on posters for bluesmen and women of the Delta—the dates went back seventy years at least, perhaps more judging from the curl and warp of the paper. The support beams were all in place—though they had a weary, weathered look of burden, as though they'd held the roof in place for nearly as long as they could manage. In front of me, a chromed record jukebox lit a gaudy rainbow of neon, though the red and green bulbs were burned out. On the far wall was a wooden platform raised a foot off the ground, and a modified bar—a sliding-top door like you'd find in a stable had been opened permanently and given a surface with two-by-fours and plywood. In the dim recess behind, an old black woman with white, unkempt hair and pitted cheeks regarded me with bright, careful eyes, a constellation of liquor bottles at her back. Between her and me were a dozen metal-legged white Formica tables with matching folding chairs, each holding a few drinkers who clutched mason jars filled with ice and colored liquid, or beer, and whose white smoke rose and mingled and turned in the air above each party, a bank of smoke mounting to the V of the roof. The black men wore white tanks and jeans and mostly stood, their bodies leaning confidently over the tables. I found my party in the rear corner: Mrs. Mason, Mrs. Hudson, and Ms. Beadle waved beckoning hands. Behind them, a tall, dark man in a black-collared shirt hovered with his fist claiming the back of Ms. Beadle's chair. When he saw me he stared until he noticed me noticing him and finally looked away. I had a general prickle of unpleasant measuring—it seemed the eye of every person in the place was on me.

I gestured in the direction of the back to indicate I needed a drink and made for the old woman, who had to be the bartender. She'd been watching me with an air of proprietary curiosity, as if waiting for me to declare the nature of my business. I obliged. "Gin and tonic, please."

She cocked her head skeptically. "Now that ain't no way to greet nobody," she said in a voice raspy and surprisingly deep. Sensing she had the upper hand, she wet her lips. "Son, my name Miz Penny Love, and I your bar-ten-dress this evening. And what your name is?"

"Oh—sorry—Mr. Mike Copperman."

She held out a wrinkled hand and we shook. "Pleased to meet you, Mister Copperman. So, you here for Big Midnight?"

"Ma'am?"

She nodded toward a wiry, gray-haired old man at a nearby table. I glanced at him. He moved from the neck, nodding his way through this point and that as he perched on the edge of a stool at the head of a circle of younger men smoking purposefully about him. "Big Midnight Benson. Our blues legend. Our man of the guitar who make the sweet sweet love come out his fingers."

"I—sure."

"Well, all right then," she said. She reached for a jar, scooped it through a trough of ice, turned a bottle of some gin with a bright label, and took the glass nearly to the rim before splashing tonic from a gun. "One dollar fifty cent for one gin and tonic."

I gave her three dollars, tipped the change, and steered the brimming gin and gin toward the table.

The ladies stood and embraced me with enthusiasm. Ms. Beadle held the hug long enough to make the man who'd attached himself to her scowl visibly as he extended a hand.

"Name D. T.," he said in a voice that seemed disproportionately small and high.

"Mike." I sat in the empty chair by Mrs. Mason and hoped to disappear. Luck wasn't with me, for Ms. Beadle immediately admired my shoes, making me explain about Pumas and was it a well-known logo and ain't the real puma's habitat in Africa or South America or where all? The inanity gave way to awkward silence, the general murmur of the place making the absence of conversation evident. I choked down a mouthful of gin, noted the distinguished finish of rubbing alcohol, and cleared my throat. "So how's the evening been for y'all?"

They all looked at me with bemusement; D. T. chuckled and then choked on it a little. I realized that in trying to be casual I'd instead managed my bad black Delta voice. I'd tried to keep Mississippi out of my inflection, but months of Delta children had taken their toll: I sounded like a black fourth grader trying to speak like a grown man. When I'd recorded a new phone message it had taken twelve tries: I'd sounded comically affected, childish, dropping y'alls and fitting to's and gone's. The ladies' chorus of "Good" and "Fine" did nothing to dull my reddening face. I was saved from further humiliation by a stirring at the stage and the snapping crackle of a microphone. Big Midnight had taken the stage and stood swaybacked, a guitar of yellow unfinished wood hanging from a shoulder strap. He tapped the microphone and then a lower mic intended to catch the sound of his guitar; then he lifted the guitar and took a few stuttering steps forward and back as if to orient himself. By the time he was settled, a hush had fallen over the room; then there was nothing but the echoing thud of the microphone.

"This song called 'What All I Got in Me Tonight,'" he said in a voice toneless and hoarse, as if he were unaccustomed to speaking. There was a squealing of strings as his knotty fingers found the frets. Then the song began with the first notes plucked hard and bold, and I knew I'd need to say nothing more this night, and I wasn't thankful for that, but for the gift of what was before me, the mournful ease of these blues. It wasn't there except for how he touched it, how he seized the get-right-on-down-to-it, flame-flicker-and-they-ain't-no-wind of it, the falling in the hush of night and only, only one last light in the dark. Here was the left-my-wom-an-at-the-crossroad and-the-road don't-lead-back-no-more, the lord-let-me-lay-my-troubles-down and the when-is-you-gone-lift-me-up and all the vital, urgent life between.

I'd heard nothing like that night at Club Sweet, and it wasn't my rising drunk, as I finished my gin and gin and had a couple more and found I'd come to be by Ms. Beadle and her hand had found my wrist, her fingertips caressing the skin with such obvious interest that D. T. had absented himself in surrender. That music sang. I have looked for mention of a Big Midnight Benson, for any proof at all that such a per-former existed or had recorded anything at all, and now it has been too long—I may have the wrong name entirely, may have made the name up or have added big or midnight or Benson, and there is no way to remember or confirm. When it was done I pulled myself from Ms. Beadle's grasp with a mumbled excuse and made my way out the door, the world spinning inconsiderately so that I stood for a moment in the lot, trying to get my feet under me. The air was cool now, with the sky spread a million stars above and the murmur of the club distant behind the door. I heard a scratch of feet to gravel and saw that D. T. hadn't left at all. He was on the far side of the parking lot, closing fast. "Hey!" he called, his voice insistent. "You! I want to talk to you."

I waited, watched him stomp for me with gravel-tossing steps, and tried to summon some protective anger, at least a straightening flash of adrenaline. He was coming to fight over his woman. I felt a panoramic inevitability take me, as if all night he'd been waving his arms at the edge of things, waiting to be noticed. He seemed so small, so very small that when he reached me and towered over me by a full head, so near I could smell the whiskey on his breath, I was surprised. "Ms. Beadle's back inside waiting," I said.

"What?" He swayed a little, puzzled.

"Ms. Beadle wants you. She's waiting inside."

His brow furrowed. Then he grinned. He was missing a couple teeth. "All right, then." He cleared his throat. I readied myself to dodge, closed my hands to fists.

"What I was gone say is you my sister boy Demetrius teacher. Mr. Coopman, right? Boy talk, talk, talk—I sure you know. He don't have no sense. But he—he like school this year. He say you teach him all kind of good thing, up in your room, and after school with them karate classes. I'd wanted to say that—that it mean something that you come all this way to teach the boy. I want to—thank you."

Demetrius was one of my favorites, a good student who often stayed after in these last months, asking endless questions about the world beyond the streets of the black side of town. I blinked, stepped forward and shook his hand, accepted his clap to the elbow and thanked him for what he'd said. Then I drove the mile home despite the drunken turning of the world, and in me there was only his thanks and the echo of those blues. All these years, and it's there still: those notes, the feel of the night, the sky a bruised black and flush with stars bright and distant. I never belonged in the Delta when I was there. I thought then that that was the fault of the place, hadn't realized that isolation is what you carry with you. Once I left, everything returned me, demanded reckoning. That night was just there, linking me for a moment in a chain whose ends rarely meet.

HARM

When I was a child, my father once took me to the park on a spring afternoon, the air flush with the scent of fresh-mown grass. I wandered the playground while he ran laps on the gravel track. I noticed a swell of voices, looked up to see my father confronting a group of black boys who were perhaps twelve or thirteen years old.

"Did you throw that rock?" he said, anger rising to his voice, and then one boy, half a head taller than the rest, taller than my father, stepped forward. "Naw, man, you crazy. Saying we done something we ain't. Stupid cracker."

My father's eyes went large as he stepped forward, him and the tall boy almost bumping, and then my father had the boy's arm, ten years of martial arts, and I knew the submission, the boy straight to the ground and my father with his wrist twisted, the others bellowing and cursing, the boy writhing on the gravel as my father held him, face expressionless, clinical. Finally my father let go and the boy found his feet, gangly and young now, yelling about calling the cops as they all backed away. My father stood and watched them until they'd left the park. Then he hurried me from the playground, his hand trembling as he held mine too hard, him walking so fast for home I had to skip to keep up, and not a word. I knew even then that he wasn't in the right, but the intricacy of such anger and shame was beyond me.

My father is not in fact an angry or violent man. He is disciplined and dedicated, a gentle, soft-spoken doctor who has worked fourteen-hour days for his patients, paying each the respect of careful attention. He has practiced medicine for some thirty-five years. Once he explained to me why he was in Oregon in family practice. This was as he came on his sixties and I was in my late twenties, and he'd begun to feel the need to explain life's disappointments, griefs, and complications. He'd planned on practicing medicine in California, had been in residency in Long Beach, at the veteran's hospital bordering the sun-baked barrio and seediest part of the strip. Seventy-hour weeks, sixteen-hour shifts and eight hours off and back on again, the tweakers, crackheads, drunks, muggings, the bad accidents off the One, night after night. I remember his face as he spoke, my father who admitted no weakness, tolerated no failure, who in the face of adversity endlessly persevered. His eyes were distant and his jaw tight as he said, "I quit the residency. I came to Oregon where you didn't need residency for family practice—packed your mother out of that cramped little apartment and drove off. I couldn't have stood another day of it."

I stared at him. This couldn't be coming from my father, the man who meditated four hours a night because he could not sleep and would take no sleep aid, then worked fourteen hours and went on a thirty-mile bike ride and ate boiled, unsalted cabbage and then did it all over again. This was the man who had been most proud of me when I won wrestling matches through sheer mental toughness, who told anyone who'd listen again and again the story of my victory: "They were bigger, stronger, taller, but he pushed them until they broke. Neck and neck through the match, and he outsuffered them," he bragged—the only time I ever heard him brag about me. "He refused to quit—and so he won."

He noticed my disbelief, cleared his throat. "Do no harm is the standard of the doctor. It can be difficult, when charged with life and death, crisis. What it was, was—it was—look. One night this fellow comes in to the ER—a drunk. His name was Leroy, an old bald drunk with no front teeth. We knew him well. He'd come in with alcohol poisoning, and we'd pump his stomach, him cussing us out. He'd come in withdrawal, and we'd have to morphine him up. That night, another resident had put him in a back room—he hadn't seemed bad. I just happened to be walking past the room at three a.m. and thought to check. He looked too still, and then I saw he'd stopped breathing. I intubated him right there on the spot, saved his life. He was with us for a couple days, even thanked me for helping him, said he was going to enter a program and get right.

"A day later, it was a hell shift, my fourth in four days, a five-car pileup and people bleeding out, a kid shot with his father's gun, an old lady in cardiac. It's four, five a.m., and all this still going and then a cop brings in Leroy and leaves him. He smells like gutter and piss, like whiskey. All these people dying through nothing they did and here I saved his life and he's back in drunk, days after it nearly killed him. He's angry, agitated. He knocks papers from a desk, points at me and screams, 'Fuck you! Fuck you bastards trying to . . .' and so on and so on. I stand there watching him, tired, with other sick, deserving people to attend to. I tell him to calm down, and he gives me the finger, holds it there right in my face. I grab him by the shoulders and sit him down to a chair, hard. Knock the wind from him, and I'm glad. I can feel he's just a frail old man, but I yank him to a gurney. Push him here and there doing my examination, rough him up a bit as I go. Take some pleasure doing so, even. And at the end he's disoriented, and I just shake my head and leave him and go attend to other patients.

"When I come back, he runs up to me sobbing, saying over and over, 'Thank God you come, thank God you come, there was a bad doctor here hurting me.' He didn't remember I'd treated him that way and left him there, any more than he remembered it was me who saved his life."

My father paused, took a deep breath. "If I'd stayed another year, if I'd had to do that, night after night—I don't know what it would have done to me. I couldn't do it. I started planning to leave the next week. I was losing the whole reason I wanted to be a doctor. To help and to heal. Do no harm."

My father did not expect it when I told him, look, Dad, I know. We can go too far, can betray our own integrity. I understand.

Though I'd never have admitted it out loud, my first year my favorite student was certainly Talika Johnson, so smart and engaged and endlessly opinionated, able to hold forth with a frown, a finger always lifted to illustrate in air just how right she was and just how wrong you were until suddenly even she couldn't hold onto her outrage and her face broke out in a huge, bright smile. Often, at the end of the day, I'd go to my mailbox and find she'd written me a letter about some injustice, often imagined or meant to manipulate me. She often wrote regarding her rival, Demetrius, who was quiet and polite, and her transparent claims often left me howling with laughter:

Dear Mr. Copperman, This is your most caring student, Talika. I had just wanted to let you know that boy Demetrius is meddling me again, saying all kind nasty things about my Mama, and also he called you a Ching-Chong-Chinaman and was speaking some Chinese words all the time you was giving him the Scholar of the Day award, and that don't seem right. I do hope you understand better now about the boy's disrespect, and will treat him accordingly.

Your Best and Most Admiring Student,

Talika

She was mercurial, however, and stubborn when she felt she was in the right, and often she would argue to the point of absurdity, her arms crossed and her hip cocked to one side and her eyes narrowed as she carried on: "Mr. Copperman, how is you gone do me like that and take away near half my recess just for talking to my cousin. She my family. It ain't fair, and it ain't right, and I ain't gone stand by and let nobody treat me like—"

And I would take another five minutes of her recess, and her cheeks would redden and she would shake with anger. Usually, she managed to restrain herself; sometimes, she'd throw a screaming fit, stomping her feet and hyperventilating, and I'd steer her to a corner and let her calm herself. When I had the time to devote to dealing with her, all was fine, but on days when the bad boys in the class were acting up and it was all I could do to sustain order, Talika melting down became a real problem, the proverbial straw, and I would lose it.

One Tuesday everything went wrong—two boys fought over a pencil, forcing the math lesson I'd stayed up until midnight planning to be abandoned. The entire day was sustained chaos, the children refusing to quiet down or focus. Perhaps feeding off that energy, Talika refused a simple request to sit up in her chair, instead slouching lower still, and when I took her recess minutes she had a fit and knocked her desk over and went into so profane a diatribe that I sent her to the room next door, and then, during my planning period, called the number I had for her home and left a message on the answering machine detailing her behavior.

After school, Talika stayed as she usually did; she'd calmed down and now was sweeping the room and humming to herself, the crisis of the day in the past now. A heavyset man in a stained white undershirt and jeans appeared in the doorway. His skin was patchy, here the color of yesterday's coffee grounds and there almost gold, and his eyes were close set and bloodshot. He didn't speak.

"I'm Mr. Copperman," I said.

He looked at me, then slowly nodded his head. "Dequarious Fenton. I heard your message calling my home."

Talika had noticed him now and stopped sweeping midstroke. She looked uneasy—I could see we were finally getting somewhere.

"Talika was disrespectful today. She talked out, talked back, and threw a fit in class. It's a real problem," I said. "She has no respect."

He nodded gravely. "I've seen her disrespect." He turned to Talika and held out his hand.

"No," she said. "You said no more."

"Give me that belt, girl." He took her wrist and pulled her to him.

I stepped back.

"No, I ain't did nothing," Talika said, pulling away. He yanked her closer, twisted her belt buckle free. The belt caught, and he tore it through the loops.

"Teach you respect your goddamn teacher." He looped the belt once so he held both ends. "Turn your black butt around."

"No, no, no," Talika cried. He swung from the shoulder.

The belt snapped hard on her side. She screamed and cringed away.

"I told you turn around." He was angry now, eyes wide, nostrils flared. He started swinging. She was crying. Her nose was running, liquid flowing from her eyes and nose and half-open mouth. She was getting hit on the legs, the back, the arm, because she wouldn't turn.

"Turn around, Talika," I said. I tried to sound calm and firm, using my best teacher's voice. I'd brought her here and could show no weakness. I wanted to puke, to turn my back. Still Talika refused to submit, squealed and cursed and sobbed.

Finally he was done. He let go of Talika's wrist and she ran behind me, buried her face in my shirt, choking and sobbing. He nodded at me. He seemed calm again, almost sleepy, although a faint sheen of sweat coated his skin from the exertion.

"Won't be having that problem again," he said. "Sure enough won't. The girl's mama and grandmamma think just because I ain't her birth father, that she don't need discipline. But she sure do."

He switched her belt from his right hand to his left and held out his hand to shake. "Glad we could deal with this now."

He was grinning, could tell from my face that I didn't have the stomach for this. I looked at his hand, took it and squeezed hard. His eyes widened. I imagined his fingers breaking one by one. His palm was sweaty from the leather. Finally I let go. He wiggled his fingers and looked at me with a hint of smile, then glanced at Talika, who was still cowering behind me. "You'll see the girl gets home?"

"Home?"

"To her grandmamma house where she stay at."

"Sure." He turned and closed the door, and we listened to his heavy footfalls recede. Talika edged back in front of me with a look of such reproach as I hope never to see again, and then she ran from the room.

She never stayed again to sweep. My principal, when I told her and asked what could be done, told me I ought to be glad an adult took enough interest in the girl to whup her. And while Talika eventually ignored what had happened and forgave me, blessed with the child's capacity to rebound, I will never forget the sound of leather to skin, or the look in her eyes, naming me guilty, guilty, guilty.

Some days, I'd give anything to be twenty-two again, to have more heart than sense and still believe that good overcomes all else. I wanted to save children from the circumstances they were born into and believed I was capable of anything. I found that I was indeed capable of anything—of doing harm to those I wanted to help, of being unable to accomplish a task as simple as getting fourth graders to stand in a quiet line. It is difficult to communicate the height of frustration I occupied, to conceive of a version of myself who could have acted as I sometimes did in the classroom—screaming at children, banging desks, tearing a child's sleeve from his shirt, tossing a boy headfirst into the hall and slamming the classroom door behind him, punching a concrete wall above a little girl's head when she spat on me and called me "China-man." Admitting how far I was pushed would be to accept the judgment that inevitably follows—how could *anyone* do such things, let alone a man who is generally calm, kind, and decent? When I left Mississippi after two years, I told myself I'd met my commitment, done my part. The truth was that I lacked the courage to stay, to risk failing another child I wanted only to help. Like my father, I couldn't have stood another day of it, or so I thought. I didn't realize I had been changed, that Talika Johnson would always be with me.

In the summer months after I left the Delta, I walked dazed through Portland city blocks, staggered by the number of people, the frantic pace of traffic, and the towers of metal and glass floating overhead. I became disoriented in malls, dizzied by the variety of clothes and shoes and electronics, the terrible volume of the new. I lapsed into long silences, refused to speak more than a terse sentence or two about teaching. My father respected this restraint; he understood that there are sins we turn from even as conscience takes its toll—a slow and painful reckoning. It has taken a decade, now, for me to let myself really remember, and finally, to begin to forgive myself.

I have been my father, terrible with rage, wanting to punish disrespect, acquiescing to violence and then flinching from what I might do if I kept on. Perhaps now I have also begun to inhabit his better self, owning up to my culpability and persisting. For though my father once threw a child in a wrist hold and was rough with an old drunk, the same man will make a house call to an elderly patient who is dying and refuse to charge him for the visit, knowing he has no money, and will tell nobody of his good deed; for though I have erred in anger and caused children to be beaten, today I teach classrooms of eager, clamorous, deserving students, grown to eighteen and having already defeated the odds in reaching college, who nonetheless require the best invitations to success I can offer them.

Atonement is a lie with which we comfort ourselves, substituting what we can do right for what we've done wrong, pretending that we can be the instruments of our own re-demption. The past is unassailable; forgiveness is all we can ever have, for others and ourselves. There is only here, now, to try to do better.

THE SECOND YEAR

WELCOME TO SUCCESS

Over the summer back in Oregon, I set out to learn how to teach. I immersed myself in education theory and methods of differentiation, consumed everything from Ellin Oliver Keene and Susan Zimmermann's *Mosaic of Thought* to Patricia Cunningham and Dorothy Hall's "Four Blocks" system, and created a scaffolded curriculum synthesizing different theories and pedagogies. I set up an installation at my father's medical office with pictures of children and an essay about teaching in the Delta and solicited donations of books, which poured in by the boxful. Then I read books geared toward best practices in creating a positive classroom culture and effective classroom management, and began to create systems and make signs and displays with poster board and Kinko prints. I convinced my mother, an architect skilled in interior design, to drive back to the Delta with me a week before school started and do a makeover of my classroom, to make it into a colorful and inviting and functional space, and she generously agreed.

We drove across the country with the Subaru packed to the ceiling and then unpacked what we had brought in the classroom, mostly boxes of books, and my mother clucked her tongue at the sloppy plainness of my room and unfurled her tape measure and sketch pad and found a vision and a plan while I swept and mopped and wiped away the dust and then began to order and mark the books according to grade level. The next day we drove to Rosewood to the nearest Lowe's for supplies, and we bought giant blue scraps of rug and great pieces of shower board and an interlocking series of folding shelves and paint trays for students to get new work and turn in old work and a hammer and nails, and then at the fabric store we purchased bright fabric and twisty-ties and wire and adhesive tape, and then at Walmart we bought pillows and beanbags and dry-erase markers and magazine holders and notebooks in bulk and the biggest electric pencil sharpener available, and then we returned to the classroom and began to work, me the grunt labor and my mother orchestrating it all, as we nailed the great pieces of shower board over the fading slate of the chalkboard to form a huge whiteboard, and threw out the nubs of chalk and filled the ledges with dry-erase markers. We laid the thick blue rug and shaped the shelves, and my mother measured and bound the fabric into a series of blue and pink and yellow arcs to form drapes to frame each window. I ordered the books on the shelves, blue and yellow and white and black and green stickers to cover the distance between the second- and sixth-grade levels, and then I set up a line of work pickup and return trays for each student, set in each one a magazine holder with a notebook within for taking notes on the book each child was reading, and sharpened a pencil and tucked it in the wire of each notebook. We propped the pillows around the edges of the reading rug and put the beanbags in the corners, and my mother's considerable work was then done and so I drove her to Memphis for an evening flight and drove back to return to work.

I taped giant, colorful letters for the word wall all the way around the classroom, and in the front above the board I secured the signs and displays I'd created concerning reading strategies that good readers apply and decoding strategies for compound words and pictures modeling the "listening learning position" and the list of three rules, the first being "Raise Your Hand Before You Speak," and the sheet bearing the class pledge I'd written right beside the American flag and the plaque put up in every classroom after 9/11, "In

God We Trust"; and then I put up the colored card system for personal behavior, with black for "Superstar," and the list of consequences for being less than super, and mounted the special whiteboard/meter for class recess time, and put up the morning math board on another piece of shower board on the wall beside my desk with a new board for "Awesome Work" and left the wall blank with expectation, and finally taped up the great glittery sign for the door that just like the year before said "Welcome to Success!" but meant it anew; and I thought that now, for the second year, I was ready. The room was clean and bright and colorful, bountiful with comfort and color and the insistence that here, in a classroom like this, only good things could happen.

Anticipating the beginning of school, I posted a list on my door with the names of all the new children. I pored over their MCT scores, asked around about this student and that, no longer assuming that ignorance allowed unbiased judgment. My class was much higher achieving than the first-year group and smaller by some accident of enrollment, only eighteen students to start: a gift. I read and repeated their names to myself over and over, Serenity and Felicia, Donte and Marvin, Demichael and Deshawn, Precious and Marquavious, Latambernique and Solomon. I spoke their names as incantation, as a promise to keep, as I set my systems in place for behavior and morning math work and reading workshop and writers' workshop. The spell of preparation must have taken, because now what I recall is not the first minutes of the first day of class, the children seated at desks and excited and a little scared of their new Chinaman teacher, being put through the paces of my first system—I kept a small silver bell by the front board, and whenever rung, it required eyes up front and hands to desk and complete silence. I must have taught the bell and practiced it, gone over the classroom rules and the card-behavior system and the recess minute meter, must have been nervous and focused, sleep deprived but wired. We must have gone over behavior in lines, over year-long goals, over the class motto; they must have been on their best behavior, though perhaps Felicia Jackson was already testing me a little with an out-of-turn comment or a slow compliance to sit up straight or keep her hands to the desk. All of that surely happened, but I cannot recall it. Instead, my only memory is of a morning during the first week, the children suddenly there in the rows of desks with raised name tags, faces all turned to the front of the room and feet tucked beneath chairs as I'd just rung the bell to signal the end to a work period. I asked a question about a math problem, waited as arms shot up, waving with waiting answers.

Hope filled those early, expectant days of the new school year. Aspiration and excitement, and not enough time yet for the routine to take; every morning was a new beginning. Children lined up outside my door, a still-asleep Felicia Jackson always there first front and center; Solomon with his big eyes and quick grin; quiet, slight-shouldered Marvin a little away from the rest of the children, still sullen with sleep, leaning to the wall with arms crossed in front of him. Around the end of the hall past the room, half a head and shoulder evident past the corner, and as my footsteps echoed down the hall as I neared the door, a furtive peek from Serenity and then a shy grin as she saw me and shuffled cautiously over to join the other children. She wanted only to come in and read, amazed and overjoyed at the scope and stock of the bookshelf, but already feared the other children, who harassed her for being quiet and gentle and especially poor. As I neared the group, the children would go silent, hitting each other on the arm so they noticed and were ready, straightening collars and pulling on packs and standing back from the door so I could let them in.

"Good morning!" I'd call in my loudest, gladdest voice, an old aikido trick of putting positive energy forth to carry the day, and Marvin would wince at the volume and Felicia narrow her eyes and mutter under her breath about how *Can't nobody know something gone be good before it start*, and I'd throw open the door and the children would push through, jostling, me calling out "Slow down!" Really, I wasn't any more patient than them: I wanted the day to flare and shine with imminence. In those early mornings of those early days of August and September, every dream seemed within reach.

I'd agreed to be a part of the Title I after-school program, Delta Horizons, which sought to offer enrichment and support and perspective to children who demonstrated potential. The teacher at Promise-Upper who administrated the program had noted my aikido program from the year before and offered me the opportunity to offer the class as a part of the program for extra money on the paycheck; I jumped at the offer. What I hadn't considered was just how much of a commitment it would be to finish the school day and go straight to teaching three aikido classes—I would try to hustle my kids out, already many not wanting to leave, Felicia forcing me to physically push her out, Serenity often nearly being locked in because I hadn't noticed her barricaded with beanbags and pillows in the corner behind my desk, head buried in a book. I'd lobbied hard to get a number of my students into Delta Horizons, and so at three-thirty I'd lock the classroom and head out with them in tow, quiet and sweet Donte content to walk hand in hand with Precious, whom he was perhaps a little sweet on, and Marvin spacey and giggly and Solomon behind all of us zigging this way and that, so that

I kept having to stop and wait for him as he lolled down the hall, goofy and clowning and laughing at his own antics. I'd finally get them to one of the Delta Horizons teachers and hurry to the boy's room and don my gi and hakama, the layers of fabric hot and uncomfortable in the warm afternoon, jog the hall toward the gym while other students free now from school and authority called out *Heee-yah!* and *Whaaaa!!!* and sometimes, imploringly from my students the year before, *How come can't everybody who want to do that aii-key-doe no more?!!!*

In the gym, my three designated mat makers were already connecting the Velcro of the tumbling mats. Tucked in the corner under the last mat, I kept a notebook with every aikido lesson and exercise that had worked well the year before, and as the red and blue and yellow mats got spread into a great rectangle, the thwap of mats hitting floor and the patter of bare feet of the mat layers the only sound, I'd try to figure out what I was going to teach, what direction to try to take the first class, knowing full well that I'd improvise, that the first group might not go well, that I should have prepared more before but had been focused on the classroom. I'd take a deep breath and let it out and raise myself on the balls of my feet and come down and find a center, heeding my own lessons about balance and poise and calm, and then the first voices of the first class of twenty children would be audible, laughter and whispering, a shuffling of feet by the outside door as the line formed up, and I'd clap my hands at the mat boys, who'd finished their work, and they'd step to the back of the mats and straighten, and then I'd walk to the corner of the gym, pull my belt tight and the front of the hakama straight, smile at the aide who'd brought the children to let her know I had them, and say, "Slowly and quietly, shoes in a straight row and a line in the back in *seiza* in twenty seconds on my count: Begin!"

The children would hurry to the back and pull their shoes and socks off quick as they could and set them straight and race for the mat to sit with backs straight and knees to the first line of mat panels and toes tucked flat underneath as I made my way to the front of the room and then sat myself in seiza facing them and continued counting, even but slow and then slower still as the last stragglers hurried to make the line, ". . . eighteen . . . nineteen . . . and twenty."

And then, after a moment of silence, the sound of the harried students breathing a little audibly as they caught their breath, I would pivot on my toes and bow low to the front of the gym as all the students bowed too on my lead, pivot again to face them, and call out as we bowed to each other to begin, *oneigashi mas!*, which we all knew meant "please do me the honor of training with me"; and we would begin our traditional stretches to my loud count there in the dim hot gym in the most unlikely dojo in the world.

Returning to the Delta was not so easy outside the classroom. After a couple of months, I'd finally adjusted to being back in Oregon, where all was comfortable and expected and I didn't stand out so much for the hue of my skin and the slant of my eyes. Now I was aware again of the stares, of the crawl of eyes always on me reminding me *Chinaman, you are not from here*. Black people at the gas station and street corner, teenage boys leaning to the front of the Sunflower food store, white women in floral prints in line at the drive-in and passing in the aisles of the video store, men in the fitness club pumping iron, stopping midset to stare, resuming with a shake of their head. The feel of eyes walking the Walmart parking lot, eyes at the Double-Quick, eyes at the bank in line in the heat, sweat beading on my forehead and eyes taking in the sweat as something new, look, Asians sweat too, that man is sweating, his yellow skin sweats, look. I could feel eyes at night as I slept crawling along my neck, an aggregate gaze lingering inches off my ear.

I craved privacy. I'd close the door to my house and draw the shades so that I did not have to look over at the Academy field or find the eyes of passing children from the ninth-grade school peering in, everyone knowing where I lived, wanting to see what the Chinaman did in his living room. I would crank the air conditioning and raise the volume on the television so that all I heard was the flat comfort of uninflected Hollywood English, and then I would grade or plan or read in the refuge of the melodramas or soaps or bad action films with bad actors, nothing but a murmur, unlike the voices that echoed through my days and through my dreams.

That year, Teach For America was in the midst of a push for corps members to effectively demonstrate what they called "Significant Gains." It seemed that every Saturday we were asked to drive to Rosedale or Piedmont or all the way to Oxford for a workshop or professional development session designed to ensure that we understood the importance of realizing "Significant Gains," a term implying that we had made an impact, reached the promised land of achievement. Speaker after speaker urged us to reach higher, work harder, be more rigorous and uncompromisingly dedicated, the stakes nothing less than these children's educations and therefore also the course of their entire lives. They listed ways we could numerically demonstrate our success, insisted that this emphasis on testable outcomes was different from the emphasis on the state tests so many of us hated within our schools—we were not to teach test-taking strategies but to realize gains of rigorous metrics defining surpassing achievement. We needed to aim high and exceed our own expectations, or we were failing our children.

None of us in our second year needed these reminders, but we were still susceptible to the rhetoric and mission, to the urgency of the message; most of us had struggled our first year, had pledged to return and do everything right. We wanted to hold graphs and statistics that said we'd succeeded, that we had been the sort of teachers we certainly hadn't been in our first year. We felt like seasoned veterans as we advised the first-year corps members, giggling behind our hands at their earnestness and innocence and greenness, feeling that now we *knew*. We went to restaurants and bars in the bigger towns after these sessions, drank ourselves blurry and blustery on the ambition of our plans, seeking the courage to ignore the doubt that coursed beneath in the distance between our aspirations and what was possible. There was a breathtaking absurdity to the scale of this mission we were on—to save the children, reform the education system, and somehow unmake the inequalities and injustices of this place in the course of a single year in our classrooms. We awoke painfully sober and went back to work all day Sunday until the late hours of the evening. We were right to be scared.

After all, we were in some of the most troubled schools in the country, far removed from the easier circumstances of most of our own origins, and our children, even the brightest of them, would have to persist through a segregated school system that offered few resources. In a series of meetings, Mrs. Burtonsen had gravely informed the teachers at Promise-Upper that our children hadn't met the proficiency standard gains mandated by No Child Left Behind, that we had to do more so as not to be deemed a "failing" school at risk of being taken over by the state. She knew that her job was at risk; she made even the veteran teachers feel that their jobs were as well. Our computer periods were no longer to be devoted to teaching technology or enrichment or literacy but rather to a computer program that simulated the Mississippi Curriculum Test and allowed our students to practice the multiple-choice test-taking strategies that we were mandated to teach. We opened the year with a school-wide rally devoted to our commitment to the test; at every meeting, we were told that our students had to test well, that we were to narrow our instruction to the benchmarks most often emphasized on the tests, that achievement on the tests was absolutely essential, that the rest of what teaching entailed—inspiration, nurturing, enrichment, encouragement—would take care of itself. So it was that in the first month of the school year, a couple of veteran Promise teachers printed off and laminated posters designed to encourage the Promise-Upper community in unified commitment to academic achievement on the Mississippi state tests and posted them on every door. They read:

"SUCCESS DEPEND ON US!"

Precious and Felicia, two of my brightest students, stood giggling in front of the sign the morning it appeared. When I came up, Felicia put a hand to my arm and craned her chin at the sign. "Look, Mr. Copperman, *we hasus* a mission!"

"What you think, Mr. Copperman?" Precious said. "*Are* it true?"

Felicia raised her eyebrows. "Can it be? *Is* we *all* up in school for to get *us an* education?"

I tried not to smile and failed, though already I was wondering if I'd offend anyone if I took the poster down; I already hated the emphasis on testing enough as it was, quietly refusing to alter my emphasis on the readers' and writers' workshop, secretly writing cryptic excuses to the computer teacher and keeping my kids in the classroom for the computer periods when they were supposed to practice multiple choice.

"Well," Precious said, nodding her head. "*It* hard to *say*. I suppose the answer *depend* on *us!*"

As it turned out, it did.

LETTING GO

Driving to school at six-thirty in the morning, the streets gray and foggy, I followed the fence line of the Academy field and then turned down Magnolia's line of two-story colonials, their high white columns draped with the red and blue of the Confederate flag. The dark windows of downtown blinked past, then I jolted over the tracks and was on the black side of town. The street hadn't changed course, only name, now Felicity, although the potholes were deeper. This side of town was already awake: black people lingered on street corners next to tilting mailboxes, leaned on rusted Chevys, and squatted on broken stoops and rotting porches. Children wandered the edge of the road trying to get lost before they found their way to school, travel bags with their books and supplies trailing behind. I drove with my windows up, but three weeks into teaching I already knew the sound of their voices, loud with bravado, knew the sound of wheels clicking on pavement.

I was the first teacher to school, but the janitor had already unlocked the doors. As I entered the fourth-grade hall I saw Felicia Jackson, my favorite, asleep against my door. She had an angular, fine-boned face and carried herself with an air of authority, as if she knew she'd be the center of attention and the proof was you were looking at her. Now it was different: she was curled on her side, chest rising and falling in sleep. Her head rested on one arm, and I smiled when I saw that she was sucking her thumb. Her face was serene, guileless. A child's face.

I scooted her sideways. She woke, yawned toothily.

"Good morning, Mr. Copperman," she said.

"Good morning, Felicia."

She stood and stretched her arms overhead. "It just so good to see you this morning, Mr. Copperman, I'm just gone have to give you a hug!" She threw her arms around me and pressed her face to my chest. I held my hands from my body, wary of the warnings about boundaries, thinking lawsuit, lawsuit, lawsuit, but reluctant to hurt her feelings.

"Shoot," she said. "Here I come early for one dead fish hug like that. Guess I'm gone have to go and get me some breakfast cause nobody like fish in the morning." She headed down the hall chuckling. I shook my head and unlocked the classroom door.

That day I taught rubrics. Felicia's head was down, and I wasn't about to disturb her. We moved to word games, one of my few successes so far. This was a new game where the kids used clues to guess a word. Felicia sat up and yawned.

"If you get it on the first clue, you're a master, but if you don't get it until the end then you need to try harder," I said. Up went Felicia's hand. She didn't wait to be called on.

"So, as it pertains to rubrics, it's a rubric in reverse?"

Pertains? I had to think. With a rubric, a lower score is worse and a higher score better; with the word-guessing game, the lower the number of clues necessary to guess the word, the better. "That's right, Felicia."

She grinned, and I turned to the board.

"Aw, go on and be like that, then."

"Felicia, I'm trying to teach."

"And?"

"And I need you to be quiet and pay attention."

She rolled her eyes.

I went on. "So, we can see that—"

"Excuse me, *sir*!"

"Yes?"

"I need to *use*." She couldn't need the bathroom—the whole class had gone fifteen minutes before.

"Felicia, if you interrupt again, I'm going to ignore you." I looked around the room at the other students. "In fact, we're all going to ignore you."

"You gone *ignore* me?"

"So, use the clues—"

"If you feeling like a pimp, go on brush your shoulders off," Felicia sang out. She was in the aisle dancing, doing the heel-toe and a shoulder-shimmy. "Felicia a pimp too, go on brush your shoulders off!"

The children roared. I recognized the words as a spin on the popular rap song. "Pretend you don't hear her," I instructed the class.

"Niggers is crazy baby, don't forget that Felicia told you, get that dirt off your shoulder," she said.

I couldn't ignore the profanity. "Stop!"

She danced away from me through the aisle. The children screamed, egging her on. She and I circled the classroom, the kids standing and clapping, until she danced out the door.

In the hall she affected indignation. "Mr. Copperman, I was just playing."

"You're going to the office."

"For what?" She put her hands on her hips and pursed her lips. "What'd I do?"

"You know what you did."

"For that? Man, shoot. Gone send me to the office for rapping and dancing." She started down the hall, speaking loud, voice echoing. "Stupid ugly little Chinaman gone send me to the office for dancing? Shoot, I gone tell Assistant Principal Winston he need to tell that mean little slant-eyed man to go back where he come from . . ."

I wanted to say something. To tell her she didn't know a

damn thing, that I was Japanese, Japanese like Pearl Harbor, the atom bomb, samurai, sushi, mother-fucking Honda, and where did she get off running her mouth? But the words sounded ugly, so I sank to the wall and listened. She kept on the length of the hall, other teachers stepping from their classrooms, pursing their lips, then closing their doors when the kids inside heard what she was saying and erupted with that country-Mississippi exclamation: "Oooh-wee!"

I lectured the kids about respect until it was time for PE. As soon as the children were to the gym I headed for the teachers' lounge. There was rarely anyone else there, but there was a vending machine and a couch.

I found Mrs. Mason sitting on the lounge couch eating a sandwich. I nodded and went to the vending machine. Someone had taped a sign on it that said "Out of Ordur." I swung for the side of the machine, remembered midstroke that Mrs. Mason was watching, and tapped the side with a hollow thump. "Sorry," I said. "I was hungry."

She smiled and held out the other half of her sandwich.

"No, but thank you," I said. "That's kind."

"So, Mr. Copperman," she said. "How's things going for you there in Room 12?"

I shook my head. "A little rough."

"That's what I heard." She pursed her lips. "Lord, Mr. Copperman, things are always rough. And things being like they are, it ain't surprising."

"What does that mean?"

She held up her hands. "Don't get me wrong, Mr. Copperman, I'm not saying nothing about you. I just mean you've got Felicia."

"Felicia."

"Felicia. You know that little girl drove Ms. Mosley clean out of the teaching profession?"

"You mean her teacher last year?"

"No, no, I mean her teacher from the lower-school years ago. That poor Ms. Samson, she got it bad from Felicia. You know she was pregnant and all. She hadn't figured to get no crazy-mean devil-child in the third grade. Felicia told her she hoped she fell on her belly and killed her baby. Don't think Ms. Samson ever forgave her that."

"I can see Felicia saying that." I blinked, thinking about what my program manager told me at the beginning of the year when he saw my roster: "You're going to need strategy, luck, and a lot of prayers."

My supervisor had come to the Delta through Teach For America some six years earlier; he stayed and kept teaching. He'd taught Felicia second grade his last year in the classroom, and he didn't sugarcoat his truth: "She is hands down the most difficult child I have ever dealt with or observed. She's brilliant and wild, has a mouth on her you wouldn't believe. She's also incredibly emotionally intelligent, knows what you're thinking and feeling, and she'll manipulate you with that. And now she's two years older. Be ready."

I'd imagined I was prepared, seasoned by a year in the classroom; clearly, I was not. I cleared my throat, addressed Mrs. Mason: "She's a lot to handle. But she's *so* smart."

"That's the truth. She's got a big brain and a big mouth. You know I went to school with Dede, her mama? That woman crazy. She was just like Felicia. Would cuss you up and down and every way if you looked at her wrong."

"I haven't met Dede."

"But you know it ain't you, don't you, Mr. Copperman? That she always been like this?"

I shook my head. "I guess I had an idea."

She motioned with a finger for me to lean closer, spoke in a whisper. "This is between you and me, Mr. Copperman. But

I know for a fact that Mrs. Sanders, Mrs. Stinson, and Mrs. Holden all refused to take Felicia this year. You know they past retirement. They told Mrs. Burtonsen that if she gave them Felicia, they were done."

That was nearly every other fourth-grade teacher. "So nobody else would take her?"

"Only somebody who didn't know better and couldn't say no," she said. She stood and smoothed her skirt. "Like you."

As Felicia's teacher, I had the right to review her file; I talked to the behavioral specialist and got access. The file held thick, multicolored sheets shuffled hodgepodge and spilling out the sides. I got my hands under it and thanked the secretary, and took the mess to the empty teachers' lounge.

There in the dim lounge I read what I could of the fat disordered file, a record of a failed and atypical education. Felicia's state test scores were near the front, and ordered by year. Mostly she was superproficient, though on one section of a test from third grade she'd literally received no points at all, which could only mean that she'd correctly chosen the wrong answer to each question. Also inside were a series of pink and yellow office referrals, sometimes in Mrs. Burtonsen's graceful cursive, sometimes in the cramped print of Winston's hand. His comments were so terse and vague as to indicate nothing, though under "measures taken" no licks had been given as with the boys I sent to the office. There was nothing to indicate the substance of the struggle in that office, the indomitable Winston facing the impossible Felicia Jackson. The reasons she'd been sent from the classroom were clear enough: "Called teacher an ugly old ho," one said. "Refused to do work. Mocked teacher to her face." Mrs. Burtonsen's notes added little: "Misbehavior: bad." "Dishonest." "Poor acting," another declared, though the word was underlined three times so that even the second sheet was pierced. Apparently I wasn't the only person who'd been frustrated with her.

What was more interesting was the evaluation done by a psychometrist, though I could see no justification for the expensive battery of tests—behavioral scales, observations, IQ, and academic skill assessments. Her IQ was at the high limit of the bell curve. I hadn't been wrong in thinking her an evil genius. Her behavior jibed well enough: she finished her math work in moments, and if I didn't call on her she either drew attention to herself or turned to torturing a classmate. Her analytical reasoning skills and ability with logical inference were off the charts. In the written evaluation of her math skills lay the only exclamation point of the tests: "Deduced and utilized algebraic principles without prior knowledge!" Her reading comprehension sheets for each passage bore no marked errors and a speed rate in triple digits, but no level was indicated except a note on the last page: "Currently unestablishable due to exceptional speed and frequent digression on all comprehension questions." I could picture it: Felicia commenting not on the passages but on the flaws of the text. When we had read "A Cricket in Times Square," she'd refused to participate in class discussion on the grounds that "nobody should waste they time on no stupid talking cat who ain't got the sense to eat no little mouse with some big fat attitude. That *stupid*." Yet she must have demonstrated something the evaluator understood, for three lines down he had written one last phrase: "Adult—or equivalent."

The psychometrist's sentences were brief, casually ungrammatical; I imagined a person accustomed to reducing situations to numbers, lifting clear and actionable conclusions from the tangle of life. The lack of idle commentary suggested it. Yet on her psychological evaluation he'd found nothing coherent, only speculation about potential "patho-logical inclinations" and a "willingness to manipulate others to get what she wants."

As if I wasn't already aware.

The librarian was the only white woman at the school, and she existed in a world of her own; I'd never observed her in the cafeteria even, or indeed anywhere except the library itself, which had its own office and bathroom. Mrs. Dudley was her name. She was in her late fifties, a stern, fine-boned woman who'd gone to fat: great bags of loose flesh hung from the backs of her arms and elbows and chin. She made up for this slackness with an air of controlled fury, her snapping turtle's neck craning constantly from side to side. She wore round red glasses that made her eyes buggy and reptilian. I'd tried to make small talk once; she'd let the words hover in the air until her silence was uncomfortable. When I asked Mrs. Mason, she laughed and said that Mrs. Dudley "might be the only librarian in the world who hates books and children."

"Black children?" I said quietly.

She shook her head. "Maybe. More likely everyone. Ms. Burtonsen likes her—says she keeps things in order." For the first months I was too busy to watch the children in the library during my prep period; no sooner had the line filed in than I was on my way out to prepare the classroom for their return. The children spoke of Mrs. Dudley with such contempt that I imagined they exaggerated; they said they were only allowed to check out books through the letter L because it "made too much work," that she spit on you when she talked and hit you with her stick and wouldn't let you ask any questions at all about the books—you were to go to the shelf and select and be immediately off. It couldn't be possible.

One day, Solomon left the library so upset that I went to him when we were back at the classroom. His eyes were red rimmed and his lip stuck out. "Everything OK?" I asked him.

He shook his head. "I'm sorry, Mr. Copperman. I shouldn't have done it. She tore up your book, even when I said I was sorry and it wasn't mine. She—tore—it—up!" When I calmed him, I came finally to the story: Solomon hadn't been able to find his library book, which was a paperback A to Z mystery. In a panic at not being able to check out, he remembered that I had the same book on the shelf, and he had gotten hold of it in the shuffle. When he handed it to Mrs. Dudley, she was easily onto him—there was no barcode or card inside. She took the book, opened it to the middle, and tore it down the spine before discarding it in the trash. Solomon kept repeating, "Right in the trash bin. The trash bin. The *trash* bin!" until I convinced him that it was OK, it was past.

The next week, I told Mrs. Dudley I wanted to stay. She sniffed a little, narrowed her magnified eyes, and cracked a metal-edged ruler to her palm, sending shockwaves up and down her arm. I went to the back and sat. The children had settled three to a table. They sat with hands folded in front of them, their books directly to their right, while she paced the room. Even Felicia was silent. Then I heard a crack of wood on flesh, and a tearful Serenity Warner yanked her elbows from the table where she'd rested them.

"Hands on the table," Mrs. Dudley said.

She went to her desk in the center of the room and shuffled papers. Then she called Deshawn's name. Deshawn stood, brought his book, and waited. She marked in his book, set it to the table, and lifted the timer. "One minute," she said. He bolted in the direction of the fiction shelves—and out lashed a fleshy arm, the ruler snapping the bare flesh of his forearm. "No running!"

I watched Deshawn at the shelves, then the next child after him. It was true—the fiction shelves turned about the wall at L, but no one braved the corner. They weren't allowed, either, to look at a book's cover or back. Once finished, they had to sit with hands folded and back straight and couldn't touch their book—they weren't allowed to read in the library. I kept waiting for Felicia's rebellion, but she seemed to have accepted this authority, for she sat expressionless, eyes shifting from me to Mrs. Dudley. She selected her book uneventfully. Only as Serenity took her book did Mrs. Dudley take her timer and paper around the lectern to better watch the checkout. That put Felicia behind her, out of her line of sight.

And then the show began.

Without moving from her chair, Felicia buried her chin in her neck and set her mouth in a look of absurd, poisonous hatred. She crossed her eyes and wrinkled her nose and gave her shoulders a perfect rounding, threw her head from side to side with Mrs. Dudley's every movement, rendering each shift ridiculous. Her imitation captured the woman's meanness and made it laughable—it was the performance of a genius mime, a Chaplin. It was clearly not the first time Felicia had played this act, for no child so much as twitched.

I saw now what went on behind my back the days Felicia was angry at me. It was all I could do to keep it from my face; finally, I exercised my adult right to avert my gaze. Had we been anywhere else I'd have laughed—yet I was afraid of the lengths Mrs. Dudley would go to. And it was justice rendered: in all her decadence, for this moment Felicia was everybody's hero.

Finally Mrs. Dudley shifted again so Felicia was visible. The last book was checked out, and I took the children off in a line. When I passed Felicia she canted her head to one side and winked. I pretended not to notice.

I began to collect Felicia Jackson tales. Stories echoed and amplified, creating new tales, each wilder than the last. Felicia had climbed a gutter to the roof and threatened to jump unless the cafeteria served catfish that day; no, she'd jumped from the roof when they'd found her catfish and driven it from a county over, but were out of hush puppies so she'd jumped anyway, but at the hospital they declared her without a scratch; no, no, she'd jumped from the roof into the middle of a panicked crowd of staff and children, who closed their eyes, screaming, but in midair she vanished, transformed into a crow that flew away cackling "Fools!" in Felicia's voice.

She'd threatened the life of her second-grade teacher with a pair of scissors; she'd stabbed her teacher with the scissors, causing her to lose a kidney; she'd cut her teacher's throat with a butcher knife and stood over her as she bled to death on the tile floor of the classroom, and they'd ruled it an accident.

She'd broken a boy's fingers by slamming them in a door; no, no, she'd bitten off his fingers including the thumb with her razor-sharp teeth; no, that wasn't it, she'd stamped the boy's hand under her shoe in a fit of pique until there was nothing left but a mangled stump.

She'd told the superintendent to go to hell; she'd told the superintendent to fuck himself in the ass; she'd told the superintendent she'd kill his family and feed the bodies to the flesh-eating rats she kept as pets in her closet at home, though nobody knew where she lived, how she lived—perhaps she was from hell itself—yes, it was the only explanation that made sense.

At the root of each story, there seemed some verifiable event—for example, the one time they sent her to "alternative school," suspension under the one-on-one supervision of a bull of a woman famed for her toughness, she'd proved too much to handle. In all versions of the story, she'd been sent back to school due to the allegations of abuse that she'd made. It was the nature and cause of the abuse that changed: in one case, they said she'd blackened her own eye by running headfirst into a door, while another version had her methodically bruising her own arm black and blue with her bare hands, and a third suggested she'd ridden the teacher so mercilessly she'd broken and actually beaten the girl, had strangled her until someone had dragged her off. The teacher had suggested it was more than justifiable, that they should've let the woman kill her and put everyone else out of their misery.

Another story I'd heard from every member of the office staff was that Felicia the previous year had screamed "Rape!" in Assistant Principal Winston's office, had thrown open the door with panicked eyes, her clothes disheveled, bra hanging from one strap—and since then, Winston would only deal with her when the door was open.

What emerged was an extraordinary and violent defiance, a nature so ruthlessly oppositional it couldn't be mastered. I believed some of the stories. What I didn't understand was how to reconcile the tales with my experience of her. In the overlap between impossibility and impossibility there had to be some truth that connected with the gentleness I could sometimes exact from her with a smile or compliment. There was something about Felicia that was worthy of effort—and I'd bring it out.

One Wednesday I drove Felicia home so I could speak to her mother. Back after her suspension for the rapping incident, at first she hadn't actively disrupted class, just refused to do her work. But at the end of the day she'd been awful. I'd tried to ignore it, but she'd been meddling poor Serenity about her old, holed clothes. Felicia whispered "smell-nasty" over and over into Serenity's ear until she got to her. I looked up from my lesson plans to find tears streaking Serenity's face as she tried to get her notes down before we moved on. It was too much. And I couldn't send Felicia to the office.

When I'd arrived at school the morning after the dancing episode, there'd been a note on school stationary slid under the classroom door. Winston was clear and to the point: "Felicia Jackson may not be sent to the office anymore. You are her classroom teacher. Deal with your children in your own classroom."

I was livid, but there was nothing I could do. I was going to have to do something myself. The school had no phone number listed for Felicia, and I still hadn't talked to her mother. I remembered what Mrs. Mason had said about Dede's imbalance but even so couldn't see how any adult wouldn't be outraged by Felicia's behavior. I had to try something.

Felicia loved the ride in the wagon. The car was a Subaru, a couple of years old, but it was clearly the nicest car she'd ever been in. She begged me to put on the radio, and watching her pleading, even remembering what she'd done, I couldn't resist. I turned up the bass. She put the window down, her head out the window screaming before I told her to rein it in or I'd turn off the radio.

"You tell me where to turn," I said. She nodded, and told me every few blocks until I realized we'd reached the school for a second time. She'd just wanted to be riding, had made no effort to direct me anywhere. I stopped the car and turned off the stereo.

"Man, shoot," she said.

"What is your mother's address?"

"You want my mama address?" She narrowed her eyes, smirked, and mumbled something under her breath. "Shoot,

Mr. Copperman, I give up. My mama stay at 647 Wiggins Road. It only five blocks from here if you go and turn on Wiggins."

She sounded pleased with herself, which just made me angrier. I threw the car into drive and drove fast, bouncing over the potholed streets.

The house was tucked into a dead-end alley off Wiggins Road. The street became packed dirt as we neared her house and I had to slow down. Ten or twelve tin trailer units were crushed together, no fences between them, each one with a little plot out front that would've been a yard if there'd been any grass. We got out of the car and walked toward the trailer. Cans and cardboard were stacked in front of her unit. Flies zigzagged the ground with an omnipresent buzz. The smell of garbage gagged me. I knocked and heard a muffled stirring inside.

The door opened halfway to reveal a fragile woman of sixty in a pink bathrobe and black hairnet.

"Ma'am," I said. "I'm Mr. Copperman, Felicia's teacher. Can I talk to her mother?"

She looked so taken aback that I wasn't sure if she was going to say anything. Then she swung the door open.

"Lord, yes, come on in," she said. "I'm Ms. Gatlin, Felicia's grandmamma."

I offered her my hand, and she took it with both of hers and squeezed. I made no move to enter. "I'd like to speak to her mother."

Ms. Gatlin stood in the doorway looking baffled. "Felicia's mama in Georgia," she said after a time. "Felicia ain't never said nothing 'bout that?"

I shook my head, heat rising to my face. "Well, let's talk then," I finally managed.

She grinned, turned, and beckoned for me to follow. "Ain't

never had no teacher come to my home. They never took no interest."

The interior was clean but sparsely furnished. An off-white couch sat across from a television tray, and an easy chair with torn upholstery held a privileged spot in the corner. There was a light fixture with room for three bulbs, but only a single bare bulb gave light. On the opposite side of the room, a boy of five or six stared at me wide eyed, his face oddly elongated. Felicia glanced uneasily at Ms. Gatlin, then went and sat cross-legged beside the boy and kissed his swollen head. I had seen a number of children like him in the Delta. A sickle-cell child. Ms. Gatlin took to the easy chair with a sigh and motioned for me to sit on the couch.

"Mr. Copperman, Felicia don't do nothing but talk, talk, talk about you. My teacher this, my teacher that. You must be doing some job over there," she said, smiling. She was missing several teeth, and the rest were shot with fillings.

"Well, I guess so," I said.

"So how's my baby doing?" she said. I glanced at Felicia. She turned her head away when our eyes met. I looked around the room and saw plastic-framed pictures of Christ along the walls, limp, green curtains, and a yellowed plaster ceiling cracked with water damage. I cleared my throat.

"Felicia's a very smart little girl," I said. "She does fine work. Brilliant work, even." I heard Felicia let out her breath. Ms. Gatlin beamed.

"I'm so glad. Felicia always say she doing well but I never know. I'll have to tell Dede, her mother. Felicia don't see Dede much, but the girl loves her mama, always wants her mama to know how well she doing."

"Yes, ma'am."

Ms. Gatlin let out her breath. "I was sure you was gone tell me Felicia cutting up again. I get tired, but that's cause it ain't easy taking care of these babies."

"I'm sure it's a lot of work." I glanced at Felicia. She was watching me intently, her face unreadable. "But I'm sure it's what's right to do, ma'am."

"What's right before God, Mr. Copperman." She shook her head. "You go to church much? You know that church there off Main, Living Faith?"

"Yes ma'am, I know. I'm kind of—*between*—churches just now."

"Well, Felicia sings just fine, she does," she said, smiling. "In the choir there. You should come hear her some Sunday."

I met Felicia's eye and winked. She looked at me with a strange intensity.

"I will when I can, ma'am. I do bet Felicia sings just beautifully."

From then on, Felicia's behavior was different. The change in Felicia wasn't a shift in character—she could be as vicious as ever, still searched for the madcap and naughty angle, the means to assert her dominance. It was simply that she turned all the force of her personality to pleasing me. Whatever had been accomplished when I sung her praises to her grandmother despite all her transgressions had formed a bond, the binding lines invisible but strong. She'd glance toward me as she went into her usual aggression, an insult on her tongue—and bite it back. She grew used to thinking before she spoke, to speaking softer; what was ingrained retreated before a new habit of gentleness, a thirst for praise. She sat straight in her chair each day, working furiously, so that I'd let her stay after school and talk. I wanted to understand her life beyond the school, at her grandmother's apartment and on the streets of this side of town. What was it like to walk those dirt roads, to linger at the edges of those chain-link fences? What was the feel of the back alley and grassed lot at midevening, the search for something bright in the coming dusk?

She didn't tell me; her stories were her own and revealed more in what wasn't said than what was. Most of her writing concerned her baby brother, Ladarious—her "sickle-cell baby," as she called him, who "can't do nothing for hisself but have these big brown eyes and this smile that like the sun come up on the edge of the sky, and who love-love-love his big sister who keep him safe." From this I understood she cared for her brother all afternoon, every afternoon. She spoke frequently of her mother, "Mama who gone a lot to Cleveland and Jackson and Memphis cause she got thing to do, but who take me down to the beauty shop and get my hair waved like them actress on TV so all the men gone watch me." She demanded less of her mother than she asked of everyone else—she took what she got. Her life on the streets was there only in passing mention, in telling detail: "Was down at them ball courts last night by Booker, where they ain't no nets cause them big dumb boys cut them down. That boy Pipe gone look at me wrong talking bout my brother slow, 'I need to leave the boy at home and bring what I got on over to the Pipe.' Pipe so fat-head and stupid he had forgot *he* the slow one in them slow class for them kid who don't know they head from a melon and they right from they left—but I told him til he *know*."

I was sure she told everyone until they knew—just as I was sure that the more she told me, the more entry I gained into her life. She pushed against everything preemptively, anticipating the strike, yet she wanted only to protect what little she had, hoping for a mother who'd be around to tell her how to be a woman, a life for her brother free from judgment. I could create a safe, bounded place, a space for her to be—herself. The possibilities unfurled in my mind: she'd pass the grade, I'd get her a talented and gifted scholarship to summer programs, she'd write a college essay so good they'd pay her way and hold banquets in her honor. Years later, I'd sit with her at dinner in some cultured city at a fine restaurant of dark, burnished wood and glittering chandeliers, she a young, successful woman and me grown into some easier life. She'd thank me for what I'd done, and I'd say to her: You did it yourself. It was always within you. And she'd smile and shake her head, biting back the disagreement that would have been there for a moment in a flash of her eyes.

I invited Felicia to help me before class, and mornings came to have a dependable rhythm: Felicia would be there at the door waiting, would embrace me with sleep-loggy slowness, and together we would prepare the classroom. The daily schedule and morning assignments had to go on the blackboard, and I needed to organize my lesson plans, collate worksheets, reread lesson objectives, and be sure the necessary student practice was available. These tasks were balanced by the dozen familiar chores Felicia began without a word: the floor needed sweeping and mopping, the rug vacuuming, every desk needed to be wiped free of fingerprints and pencil-lead smudges. This work was comforting, the rituals created the day ahead, and, too, there was a satisfaction in working with Felicia, who threw herself into each task. Sometimes I would pause and watch her at work, incredulous: there was no bristle now, nothing but dedication to what she'd been asked. She polished the floors until they shone; the desks were in undeviating rows, the worksheets neatly stacked. There was nothing she did without care as I wished. Sometimes she'd nod in the direction of a task she'd completed with special pride—the spines of every book straight on the shelves, perhaps—and blush with aw-shucks satisfaction, her face aglow.

Mornings I'd talk to her, if what I had to do required less of my attention. What was her favorite subject—math, of course, 'cause it just make sense. I'd pulled an Algebra II textbook from a bin of resources at my program's office, and mornings when I had time, I'd start her on a lesson, needing to explain only once, and tell her to work through it by day's end; usually that meant she'd finish by the time the rest of the class had finished the morning math sheet. Other mornings, we'd talk of the books she was reading—she favored material too adult for her, had gotten her hands on Lois Lowry's more mature books and S. E. Hinton's *The Outsiders*, which she loved more than anything—"That the way it go, Mr. Copperman," she declared. "You got to fight. Ain't no room to do nothing else."

I insisted she'd missed the point, that the boys had been harmed by the violence. But she scoffed and said, "So Johnny was supposed to stand by and let Ponyboy get hurt?" I said there was plenty of room to do a lot else, and she suffered my diatribes on the benefits of nonviolence with skepticism, waiting for me to finish before saying, "Well, that do sound nice, Mr. Copperman. Maybe that how it is back in San Francisco."

I'd say, no, no, that's how it was right here in Mississippi— this was where Dr. King made it all happen.

"And what happen to Dr. King?" she said.

I blinked, and her eyes flashed a little, and she added quietly, "Mmmhmm. And why it is that them white childrens don't come up in this school, and them white folks have all that cotton and all them fine, fancy houses?"

I stood, trying to think of what to say about the measured progress of history, the necessary sacrifices, the pace of possible change.

"Yep," she said. "That what I thought."

She liked best to talk about what she was going to do: "When I finish up in this school, and all them schools, I'm gone go as far as I can," she declared. "Gone see the world. See an ocean with some palm trees. Go to that Japan, where your people come from, and they eat with them little sticks."

"Some of 'my people,'" I said, laughing.

"Sure," she said. Japan was a new development for her—before she'd wanted to go to Spain, Mexico, New York, the North Pole.

"Where else?"

She glanced out the window as if seeking direction, then looked at me. "Where you gone go?"

I chuckled. "You mean, when I'm not teaching here anymore?" It hadn't occurred to me that she was aware I'd leave. In fact, it hadn't occurred to me in a while that I'd ever be anywhere else at all.

She nodded once, her gaze on the world outside the window, where the sun was just clearing the angled tin of the roofs. She was serious.

I cleared my throat. "Well—back out West, I suppose," I said. "To San Francisco, or Seattle. Portland."

"Is it nice out there?" She was still watching the sun, a hovering orb in a pale sky.

"It's—well . . . it's real different."

She looked at me, her gaze unusually piercing. She spoke quietly. "That sound good," she said. "West."

I let the direction be, turned back to the work at hand. Felicia lingered at the window and returned to wiping desks.

Some ideas didn't bear explanation, like how little elsewhere meant: The West was like London, the North Pole was to Japan as San Francisco was to Spain. All were equally distant.

Late November with its heat dulling to December, Christmas decorations appearing around the town, ribbons and tinsel, plastic elves and ruddy-faced, bag-bearing Santas with whole fleets of reindeer. Christmas lights dotted every house, except those on the black side of town that lacked, perhaps, any electricity. Blond-haired, blue-eyed baby Jesus was in the manger, complete with hay and horses, on the lawns of no less than four colonials on Magnolia—there was no forgetting this God. I saw no similar enactments on the black side of town—there, the holiday seemed more candy canes and snowmen than Mary and the great old white-bearded wise men. The black churches had decorated tastefully—now a bank of lights, but mostly ribbon—and I wondered, for a second, about Christmas plays. Were my children playing a darker manger scene on Sunday? Carols crackled tinnily from the speakers at the Grace Food Store and were poised, too, on the lips of my children, who dreamed of a white Christmas but had never seen snow. I saw Felicia sitting in her chair singing to herself, then saw her leave off. "What's wrong?"

She glanced at me, then said, "You know that song," and sang the first phrase of the chorus, "Si-lent night, hol-y night." Her voice held the notes, throaty and tremulous; she could sing.

"Sure."

"Well. Why is it gone claim to be a 'silent night,' when singing that part make the most beautiful noise? Ain't nothing silent 'bout it."

I grinned. "So it should be: - - - - -," I waited five beats, "night, and that would be better?"

"Naw. Maybe it like this: the sound that sung, it make you

feel like you do when it a silent night. Like," and she sang it again, slower and gentler: "*Silent night. Holy night. All is calm. All is bright.* Like that. It ain't that they no noise—it about the way them words and music make it big and quiet and still, cause Jesus there."

I had no comment on Jesus being there or not. I nodded. "Maybe you're right," I said.

She shook her head. "*Of course* I'm right, Mr. Copperman. I'm always right."

I let this be as well, unwilling to contradict her confidence.

In unselfconscious moments, Felicia revealed far more than she knew. Some mornings down the hall, I could catch the distant echo of song, her voice clear and high, and I'd stop, watch her there sitting with her back to the door, head tilted to the ceiling and eyes closed as she released the glory of the church to the empty classroom. "Amazing Grace" and "This Little Light of Mine" let free in the dim morning, for no reason but the song. She was fighting no battles and impressing no one but me, because she didn't know what she was doing, and the songs had nothing in them but the grace she provided. Once she heard me, she'd quit midnote. She didn't like to be unguarded.

"Why it is you don't sing?" Felicia asked me once, in the afternoon, music on the radio and me stepping a little in time with it.

"Because I can't hit a true note."

She shook her head, disbelieving.

"Look," I said, and launched a "Row, row, row your boat" verse not sung so much as warbled, squawked, and flatted, so that by the end Felicia was bent double with laughter.

"Man, you is BAD, Mr. Copperman," she finally said. "Don't nobody in you family sing?"

I thought of my father's voice, breaking with every note

on a car ride, the echo of my mother's laugh, *good god that's awful*. "No," I said. "No, nobody does."

"My Mama don't sing no more," Felicia said. "She say singing for the birds. But my Grandmamma do. She sing real nice."

"As do you," I said, watching her blushed smile, face averted, knowing she'd been waiting all the while for the compliment.

Christmas zeal intensified as we came toward break. Down in the well of the bayou, someone tugged a barge out with guy wires of yet another full manger scene, an exultant Joseph and Mary kneeling over the little, pink son of God. Teachers had children making candy canes and snowflakes and construction-paper snowmen.

I followed their lead, had my class write a paragraph about what Santa ought to bring them. Solomon told me that Santa was going to bring him sixteen Escalades, all in a row; I smiled and didn't inquire how he was going to drive more than one at once. Deshawn wanted the new Nelly, "cause it getting cold in here," and also some Snoop "for schizzle"; I decided that his spelling of "schizzle" was correct, however Mr. Dogg had intended it. Serenity wanted, oddly, a "painthouse"—later, I found she had meant "penthouse," though where she'd gotten the idea I couldn't imagine; she characteristically refused to explain. Felicia hid hers from my sight when I passed, playing coy, as she often did; finally she brought it to me at my desk. "It kind of dumb," she said, turning it facedown and retreating to her desk and studiously facing the front. I turned it over. "Someone to love who gone love me back."

We made it through the last day, and the children flew out the door calling "Merry Christmas!" and were gone in a sugared rush: I'd brought them cupcakes. A dozen students had surprised me with cards, some store-bought from their parents and some handmade from my own construction paper. Felicia had presented me with a strawberry pie that she'd made with her grandmother; as she made the gate, she turned back to me and pressed into my hand a tiny, gift-wrapped package, and with a shy smile sprinted out the gate. I unwrapped it slowly; within was another scrap of paper that said, "For Mr. Copperman. Love, Felicia," and a thin silver chain bearing a cross. It was finer than the sort of chain you might buy at a dollar store; there was no telling how she'd come by the necklace. It was heavy, solid. I slipped it into my pocket for safekeeping.

On my way home, I turned by the bayou. There was something irresistible about it, the place that took everything discarded and washed free. The green-scaled surface was swirled with oil-slick, orange and yellow in the patchy light, and pieces of trash often floated in the middle, unnatural blossoms waiting to waterlog into the mud. I distrusted it and was drawn to its life: the cottonwoods in leafless bristle against the sky and below the mirroring reach of the cypress; the bird in the undergrowth, unseen, but crying a constant hee-hee-hee, as though to both mourn and mock; the stirring at the surface that indicated the inestimable happenings below. The bayou took everything.

Today it had something new: the floating manger scene was down. I pulled to the side. The barge had tilted a little, so Joseph and Mary were now no longer gesturing skyward in gratitude but staring down at their own reflections. And then I realized what was truly wrong: The baby Jesus was under water. I could see the outline of the divine features interred in murk; one little hand cleared the surface, seemed to beckon with tiny white fingers, though it was in fact the water's sway. There was something terrible about it, even to my un-Christian sensibility, but there was nothing to be done, so I drove on.

On Monday I arrived at school at six forty as usual. As I opened the hall door I knew that something was different—and sure enough, down the dark corridor there was no Felicia at the door. I listened to see if she'd gone to the water fountain or the restroom. Nothing: the hall was still, the quiet palpable. In the room I flicked on the lights, felt again the lack of company. Perhaps she was sick. She'd never missed a day she wasn't suspended for—and it had been some months since she'd been in any sort of trouble. I went about the usual preparation—the schedule, the morning sheets, the graded work returned to boxes. Then I turned myself to the work she'd have done, cleaning the boards, vacuuming the rugs with the little manual vacuum, sweeping off the dust bunnies.

Other kids began to arrive after seven thirty, and I could see in each of them an immediate recognition of her absence—a searching glance about the room, a puzzled nodding of the head before they went about putting up their packs and lunches and getting to their work. I'd already marked her gone when the door flew inward, slammed once against the far wall, and rested half-open. Felicia ducked her head about the jamb, hair pulled by two neat red bows into two immaculate buns, as though she'd spent the entire morning tightening the knots just so. When she saw me her face opened to her beaming, toothy grin, and I smiled back, honestly glad to see her. She stepped through the doorway with all eyes on her.

"Morning, Felicia," I called. She smiled even bigger, eyes flashing impishly, and started forward, then jerked to a stop as if she'd come to the end of a cord binding her behind. The smile retreated, her expression suddenly unreadable, though turmoil was evident in her eyes. She remained poised there, straining forward and being drawn back. Then she lifted an accusatory finger.

"Chinaman!" she spat, each syllable twisting her mouth in disgust. Then she bolted back through the door. I stood, as paralyzed as the class, who regarded me with shock and recognition, as if waiting for me to don a straw boat-hat and do unspeakable things. In the silence that followed, Felicia's footsteps pounded down the hall. Then there was a ripping and tearing. I hurried to door. Mrs. Mason had Felicia by the elbow. On the floor was a pile of papers and posters, torn and tossed to the ground, ragged pieces of them still hanging from the wall. As Mrs. Mason steered her toward the office, Felicia twisted her head and met my eyes. She had no expression. She just looked.

Eventually, what had happened became clear: Dede had returned to gather her things before departing for Georgia for good, leaving Felicia and her little brother to live permanently with their grandmother. She'd left with her boyfriend (whom Felicia didn't get on with), and she'd told Felicia, who'd begged to go with her, that she didn't ever want her again, that she'd never wanted her at all. Felicia was suddenly adrift; she had real interest now in my praise, seemed to find it unbearable given her mother's betrayal, a lie when the truth about her was that she deserved to be abandoned. She made no pretense now of kindness—it was Felicia against the world. She was suspended after tearing the hall papers and then so wild in class that I sent her to the office again and again, made sure she went directly to Mrs. Burtonsen since I couldn't send her to Winston. After a couple of incidents, and a couple of Felicia's absurd tongue lashings, Mrs. Burtonsen told her it was her "last strike." A day later, Felicia was back in my classroom with a simple warning: the next time I sent her to the office, she was done for good. "Don't be bashful about sending her on, now," Mrs. Burtonsen said, meaning really, it was time to let Felicia go; Mrs. Burtonsen didn't understand the burden she put on me by making it my decision, allowing me weigh my own endurance for abuse against Felicia's final chance.

For weeks I tried everything I could to keep from sending Felicia to the office. She destroyed my classroom, orchestrating fights, insulting everyone, humming during instruction, making children cry several times a day; I couldn't get through a lesson without a dozen interruptions. I sent her to other teacher's classrooms, but soon enough that had to stop because she was disrupting their teaching as well. I couldn't bear to lose her, but it was obviously unfair now to the rest of my kids. Solomon Simpson summarized the sentiment clearly:

"As long as she back, Mr. C, can I stay home?"

One day when I sent her to the hall to cool off, I turned quickly to the class and told them how we needed to be kind to her, that while we couldn't control her behavior, we could control ourselves. If someone else lashes at you, I told them, you don't have to respond with violence. "An eye for an eye just makes the whole world blind," I said, invoking the Gandhi of last resort.

"But if you let them poke *both* you eyes out, then *you* the blind one," Solomon interjected. I had no reply; he was right. I'd spent all year letting Felicia poke at me, and now I was asking everyone to sacrifice themselves.

I couldn't stop. I broke out every trick I had, cooed, coddled, glared, winked, danced, cajoled, offered rewards and took away privileges, whispered in Felicia's ear and yelled at her in front of the class. As the weeks went on, there was more frustration and less nuance. During my planning period one day, Solomon imitated me at the front of the room, waving a whiteboard pen and pounding the desk for emphasis:

"Felicia Jackson, that's enough out of you! I already asked you to stop being terrible to everybody in the world six other times today! It's not OK to poke Serenity in the back of the head, kick Solomon in the shins, all the while meddling Serenity and mocking me behind my back all at the same time all day every day! I don't appreciate being called a Ching-Chong Chinaman ought to go on back to China and fry me some rice! No, don't even talk! That's a consequence! That's another consequence! No, I don't discuss consequences with fourth graders! Go on, GET OUT OF MY CLASSROOM! GO! I said, GO NOW—No, no, wait, I forgive you all those consequences. Never mind, sweetheart, you're a GOOD student. Stay and keep on hurting everybody and their learning . . ."

I stood listening, unsure whether to laugh or cry, recognizing the accuracy of the satire yet still not knowing how to give up on Felicia. That afternoon, when I asked Felicia to sit down and she let out a shriek, slammed her hands to the desk and began cussing me out, it was over. I walked her to the office with a referral, and as we stood in the office lobby she went sweet, trying again to get me to back down:

"I'm so sorry, Mr. C, it won't happen again," she said, sniffling for effect. She looked up at me with her big eyes, her lower lip a little stuck out. "It's just so hard right now."

I listened to her apology, settled to the seat next to her and put my hand to her arm. I talked quietly and earnestly, told her one last time about the consequences of the choices she'd made. Finally, I handed the referral to Felicia and stood. As she saw that I really was going to leave her in the office, a final abandonment that in a way she'd sought now for weeks, a sneer took her face. She spoke in a syrupy and sarcastic voice:

"Well, if that how it is, bye bye then, *white boy*," she said. The office staff actually gasped—though Felicia would stomp her feet and wail, even call me names in anger, this was something uglier.

She looked me in the eye and slowly tore the office referral in half, then into pieces. She nodded at the door as she tossed the referral into the air. "I said, go on and leave now, *cracker*."

The cold calculation stunned me, for the purpose of calling me cracker was as simple a declaration as could be made: you're nothing but enemy to me. For nearly six months I'd poured everything I had into helping Felicia—she'd drained every ounce of patience and compassion I possessed. As the costs mounted, I'd borne them with what little I had left to sacrifice: my own self-respect, all the other children's well-being. Watching my face from her desk, the secretary, Mrs. Hamilton, cut in gently:

"Do go on now, Mr. Copperman. There's no more you can do here with this ugly-mouthed little girl."

Soon enough there proved to be nothing anyone could do. Felicia was put in the district alternative school for extreme offenders—children who were involved in serious violence on school grounds, or those who brought knives or other weapons to school. There, one man looked out for only four children at a time. Within the week she had been expelled from the alternative school after calling the alternative school teacher a "four-eyed pervert" and threatening to allege that he'd sexually abused her. The superintendent moved her to the only place that remained: the District In-School Suspension (ISS), where she was put with other "children" as old as twenty. When the ISS teacher came for Felicia's work, she told me how Felicia had dealt with a six-foot-tall eighteen-year-old also in ISS—she put a hand to her hip and waved the other in the boy's face and said: "Boy, you ain't *nothing*, and you ain't never going to be nothing. You so stupid dumb kids come around you to feel like they smart enough to live. Ugly big-headed *black boy*. Go on try and do something and see what gone happen to you. Stay out of *my* face!"

Three days later came the news that Felicia had been kicked out of ISS. Determined to get back at the ISS teacher for some slight, she'd methodically bruised and scratched her own arm, then accused the teacher of abuse—an old trick of hers. She was taken to the police station, where the police examiner determined that the injuries were self-inflicted, but the teacher refused to take her again. She was out of options, out of places to go.

A month later, I met with Felicia's grandmother, Ms. Gatlin; the district psychologist, Mrs. Blumenberg; and a number of other Promise district officials in the library after school. The purpose of the meeting was to review a behavioral evaluation that a psychologist had done. She'd interviewed me, had me fill out a number of evaluative behavioral scales, had personally evaluated Felicia's behavior in direct interviews, and had administered a number of intelligence tests. The results were expected: her intellectual potential was literally off the charts in logical and mathematical reasoning. In terms of her behavioral issues, she'd demonstrated "considerable and serious antisocial behaviors." "People with profiles like this, to be frank," the psychologist said in her white southern lilt, "are the people who all too often end up in prison—smart, capable of being manipulative. Folks who have, for whatever reason, stopped caring when they hurt others."

"Well, sometimes that's Felicia," Ms. Gatlin admitted. Perhaps it had been a difficult set of months for her, too—she looked much worse than the last time I'd met with her, the skin around her mouth and eyes sagging with anxiety, her eyes sunk deep in bags, her voice hoarse and difficult to understand. She had brought Felicia's brother to the library and hollered directions at him every couple of minutes if he was getting into things she thought he shouldn't.

"Felicia needs long-term care," said Mrs. Burtonsen, reaching across the table to take Ms. Gatlin's hand. "The kind of help that we can't give her."

The district officials went on to outline a plan to get Felicia into an outstanding long-term care facility in Saint Louis, Missouri, for behaviorally disturbed children. A year-long residential program, the facility had its own school and was nationally recognized as professional and effective. All it would take was Ms. Gatlin contacting the facility, and the district would pay Felicia's way.

"But now, Dede told me, 'don't go signing nothing,'" Ms. Gatlin said. "She say, 'I'll send for my babies from Georgia,' that what she told me for to do. And I'm fitting to take care of these babies."

Everyone at the table sat silent at this declaration. I'd overheard the district officials talking before the meeting and knew that Felicia was to be expelled from the district. Once out, there was no telling how she'd be able to go to school; she couldn't simply transfer districts. At one point during her alternative school stay, an attempt had been made to transfer her to the Rosewood School District. Her reputation had apparently spread west down highway: they'd heard *plenty* about her, they said, and wouldn't accept her under any circumstances.

"Ms. Gatlin," I said, taking her hands across the table,

"we've talked a lot. You know that I care a great deal about Felicia."

"Yes sir, Mr. Copperman, you've done what you could, and I do appreciate you," said Ms. Gatlin.

"Then you'll know I'm speaking from the heart. I'm terrified for Felicia. Dede won't come back for Felicia and take her to Georgia, really, isn't that the truth?"

Ms. Gatlin paused, finally nodded her head grudgingly.

"So Felicia will stay with you, and she'll come back next year. And if she doesn't get help, if something doesn't change—"

"Ms. Gatlin, what Mr. Copperman's trying to say is that the district and the school have done everything possible. Do you understand that?" said Mrs. Burtonsen gently. "If you say no, then there's nothing more that we can do."

"Please," I begged.

Ms. Gatlin looked overhead as if some convenient divinity might intercede. Her eyes found her grandson, who had settled in the corner now, smashing two toys together with vigorous sound effects, his face long and strange, the pooch of his bare stomach protruding from his too-small shirt. "That Ladarious. That boy take a lot out of you. Felicia, she love her baby brother. She take care of that boy."

There was a long pause as I looked at her and she looked at Ladarious, the only sound being him calling, "Woosh! Woo! Whee!"

Ms. Gatlin crooned to him: "Shhhh. Hush, boy. Hush."

When she'd quieted him, she was wistful and resolute. She leaned toward me, put her hand on mine. "Mr. Copperman, they's my babies, is what they is," she said quietly. "They's all I got. Can't you see that? They's my babies."

There was nothing more for me to say or do—it wasn't my

place to distinguish between love and selfishness, to determine who'd suffer how. I could insist—perhaps I could even bully her into agreement. Yet I lacked the conviction to claim to know.

I said nothing else.

I let Felicia go.

Later, despite her grandmother's reluctance, she actually *was* sent to another facility for behaviorally disturbed youth, in Hattiesburg—and then sent back within a week: they didn't know how to handle her combination of acuity and defiance. Recently, I found her social media page; whatever went on in the ensuing decade, Felicia Jackson does not appear to have completed school. As of the year before the printing of this book, she was working at the Sonic Drive-Through in Promise, Mississippi.

It is hard to recapture the idealistic fervor I had back in the Delta, before I knew the impossibility of undoing history and injustice by benchmark met and lesson learned. Yet whenever I think now of that feverish year with Felicia, I cannot help but see her as she might have been: shining with rare possibility. I didn't understand that she was burning through that potential at an unsustainable rate, flaring out. I saw only the brightness—it was blinding, even glorious.

When I picture her now, everything is impossibly symbolic. I imagine her in a photograph I took the day I brought my camera to class. The photo itself was lost when my camera and computer were stolen years later, but I remember the occasion of the picture and the frame itself. Felicia had taken the globe on my desk and detached it from its base. She clutched it like a volleyball at her chest, poised to serve. She stood with her back to the window, the day blindingly bright, so that over one shoulder light poured white and erasing, leaving only the dark silhouette of the globe, its oceans and continents spreading beyond her fingers. She was grinning, her eyes bright with mischief and confidence, for she knew full well she'd found a way to get my attention—that though I'd be angry she was playing with the globe, I'd have to take a picture with her cradling the world, because the gesture was perfect. Everything was in her grasp.

ANSWERS

After only a matter of days without Felicia Jackson, I started to notice changes in the children. There seemed to be a new quality to the play of some of these boys, who could with a glance communicate an entire plot: you raise your hand and I'll throw the spitball and you'll point at someone else and say they did it and then we'll all shrug and look innocent. It wasn't that they were worse behaved but rather that they seemed more fully themselves, gentler and kinder and sillier in their antics. Solomon, living now in a universe without the need for Gandhian restraint, was a joy to watch, hand shooting in the air at every question, anticipating every direction, hanging on my every word as if memorizing it. He began to ask incessant questions: Why it is the bookcase on the right side of the room? Why it is zero the first number on the number line and how can you have a number that mean there nothing there? How it is Mr. Copperman can drink so much coffee (my seventy-two-ounce Bubba keg filled to the brim each day) and not have to go to the bathroom all the time—is Chinamen from Japan made different, or do you just hold it and hurt all day long, Mr. C? I realized, too, the unassuming but no less acute need of those kids who'd been the easiest but didn't declare themselves in bold, like Serenity Warner in her tattered and dirty uniform, who every day made herself a barricade of pillows to read. She'd never arrived early before, not with Felicia there; now she was waiting at my door every morning, her little brother Willie in tow, and while he swept the room and cleaned the chalkboards and vacuumed the rug, she'd read in the walled corner, tongue tucked to one side of her mouth, eagerly taking in other lives and stories, and she'd talk to me now with less reserve than before about how much she liked "happily ever after"–kind stories, which seemed the sort of stories there mostly were on the shelves, how she wanted to know if that was the books or if that was the world everywhere but here. The classroom was easy to manage, all the students easy now with themselves, beaming at my attention, which I had now to give. It was as if Felicia's intensity had held us all captive, and now freed, the children had suddenly been made animate.

I did less well. Some days I felt Felicia as a shadowy hovering off my shoulder, a guiltily abandoned responsibility. And now there was new regret in seeing what I'd allowed: Felicia had taken everything I had and left little for the rest of the children. I'd let her monopolize my attention, had chosen to let her terrorize the class. In refusing to let her fail, I'd done harm to everyone else, and here was the evidence: every one of these children deserved my attention and blossomed now in her absence. It was high spring, brilliant green shoots beginning beneath the dead grass of the kickball field, hard rain broken by streams of sun, the air growing in heat and humidity. There were still two months of school left; two months left to get these kids where they needed to be, now that I could actually teach. I threw myself into the work. Here, now, I would make it up to all of them.

In professional development, a veteran teacher had shared a unit on poetry; I'd taught it the year before exactly as it was written, but now I adapted it further and found that I had a class full of poets, the dialect that was a handicap on the state writing test suddenly eloquent, even profound, in explaining their lives. We did a metaphor exercise for past, present, and future; the result was striking. Solomon's poem was at once odd and precocious: "My past something you want at the store when you ain't got no money or friends to buy nothing for you."

"How about your present?" I asked, looking over his shoulder at his sheet.

"Shoot, Mr. C, can't you give a POET a chance to write his lines before you ask for answers?"

I grinned.

"My present," declared Solomon, eyeing me a little slyly, "is a classroom where they ain't no mean girls who gone meddle folk and ruin they day."

I averted my face so that Solomon couldn't see me wince.

I called Solomon "Caboose" because he always trailed at the end of the line, bouncing along behind everyone else. He had a huge "bobblehead," as his teacher the year before had affectionately called it, and big inquisitive eyes, his expressions pronounced and decisive; his small body was badly controlled, as if delayed in executing his brain's directives, and he constantly dropped pencils and papers and books and ran into desks and doorways. He was also superverbal and perceptive: you could hold an adult conversation with him, could get him to make inferences that should have been impossible from a ten-year-old. He was often a mess in the classroom, hanging upside down in his seat, making burbling noises in the back of his throat, and tearing pieces of paper to bits and chewing them together into huge, sticky wads. But he was a perpetual and hilarious ham, endlessly trying to amuse, and I couldn't say I didn't like it. When he showed me his "present" line, it was intended only to please: "My present a birthday party where my man-teacher come and bring all kind gifts and a big brass band."

I praised it—he meant it sincerely, with candles and confetti and the world's biggest tuba.

One morning, I noticed that Solomon had a black eye and was silent and sullen; when I took the kids to computer class, where they played an automated "test prep" game with the computer teacher, I pulled him from the back of the line and asked him to come back to the classroom and help me. He closed his eyes for a moment as if steeling himself for some ordeal, then nodded and followed me to the room, where I set him to sweeping, wiping the boards, and handing back graded work. He worked listlessly, lolling from one task to another, wincing now and again as if he hurt. I watched from my desk wondering how to approach him—who had beaten him, and why? I had a list of cards I kept with parental information and notes from calls; I pulled his information to refresh myself. Yes. This much I remembered: only a mother, her last name different from his, Latricia Wilkins, a round, nervously bubbly woman who'd worn a thick caking of makeup. She'd affirmed everything I said as if she'd noted it herself, so that when I mentioned that Solomon was "talented and curious, and full of good questions," she'd say something like: "I think Solomon do got a talent for to be curious," as if to pacify me as quickly as possible by showing how thoroughly she agreed.

What she was like at home I didn't know, but she seemed kind enough, and Solomon had certainly never shown signs of abuse. Of course, there was a first time for everything. She could have a new boyfriend, or be caught up in something bad; or perhaps she had nothing to do with any of it, and Solomon had fallen, had an accident outdoors, been goaded into a fight, though he wasn't the aggressive type. He was filing papers now, shuffling like an arthritic old man to each box and laying the paper inside slowly. I was used to his irrepressible boisterousness, kept waiting for a comic turn, a sudden quip, but he kept on, one sheet and the next, wincing sometimes as he leaned in. "Solomon?" I said.

He spoke without turning. "Sir?"

"Are you all right?"

His head lowered and he said nothing; I went to him, saw his shoulders shaking. I put my arm around him and squeezed gently. "Hey. It's OK. It's all right."

At this he cried harder, turned his head into his sleeve. I propped up his thin frame and repeated: "Hey, it's fine. It'll be OK."

When his sobs subsided I went to get him tissue, and he blew his nose hard and sank to the reading rug.

"Want to tell me who beat you up?"

He shook his head.

"Because I'm a teacher. I can maybe—help." I sat on the reading rug facing him and put my hand to his elbow. "You can tell me about it."

He sniffed and wiped his nose on his sleeve and looked at me with tear-reddened eyes. "It won't help none."

I let this sit for a moment and then cleared my throat. "It wasn't an adult, was it?"

He shook his head. "No, sir."

"Not at home?"

"No."

At least no need to try to involve Ms. Burtonsen, who was unlikely to be able to do anything anyway. "Well—if you need to tell me about it, now, or later, you go ahead, all right?"

He nodded, dabbed at his face again with his sleeve, and looked to the ceiling. "Mr. C, is it true that if you talk too much or look funny or don't act the same as everybody else, nobody ever gone like you?"

I scooted so I was shoulder to shoulder with him and canted my head at the same angle as his. "I'll just sit and look like you for a while, and let's see."

He started to grin, stopped himself, looked at me again with my lips puckered up and my brow furrowed and arms crossed, and giggled. "I don't look like that!"

"Do too," I said. "But I like you anyway."

He smiled.

I cleared my throat. "You know, Solomon, I was always short and too into books and looked different from everybody else. And while it wasn't easy, today people like me fine."

He nodded to acknowledge the advice, but slowly enough to show he was skeptical. Then his eyes fixed on something across the room. In front of the cubbies where students put their bags and coats, the flag hung at a forty-five degree angle, half-curled so there were mostly stars visible, then a flicker of stripes as the end swayed a little in the breeze from the cracked rear window. Solomon saw that I was looking where he was, spoke without moving his head. "What you looking at, Mr. Copperman?"

"The flag."

Solomon said, "Me, I was looking at you cubby, Mr. Copperman. Where you got your same old lunch."

For weeks, I'd been so rushed in the mornings, all I'd had time to pack for lunch were plain slices of bread, a choice that hadn't gone unremarked on by the children. "Are you hungry?"

"Naw." He got a sly look on his face. "Can you get it for a second?"

I stood and retrieved the plastic bag filled with bread and held it out to Solomon. "Have some if you're hungry."

A smile burst over his face, and then he was laughing so hard he almost choked.

"What?"

He held up a hand, laughed and laughed until he could choke it back, still grinning hugely. "It just—what you have for lunch today?"

I glanced at the bag. "Bread, of course."

"Mmm-hmm. Well, Mr. C, I just glad you got you *daily bread.*"

He laughed again, and the sound was so good to hear that it was possible to forget, as he seemed to now, the purple bruise at his jaw, the dark swell of his right eye, and his raw scabbed elbows and wrists, which was the price he paid here for being bright and different.

One spring Friday night, I went to dinner with my roommate, a fellow teacher at Promise-Upper who was also named Michael and who was six-foot-two and black. We accompanied two female corps members who taught in Rosewood. March had been a long month, kids' behavior getting worse and our own patience worn thin and our program managers forcing us to meet every weekend to stress the importance of finishing strong and so living up to our goals; we were exhausted and giddy with sleep deprivation and the freedom of a weekend with no commitments. The girls told us they were going to "dress up"; Michael convinced me to pair a collared shirt with jeans and a blazer, and off we went to meet the girls in Rosewood. The restaurant had been recommended to us as being "very white, but excellent," and it was called Delio's; the "very white" description might have given us pause, perhaps should have, except that most places we frequented in the Delta when we went to Oxford or Jackson or Memphis for the weekend were also "very white" but tolerated us. The decor was surprisingly ritzy and modern, with dark red walls, silver sculptures, and elaborate flower arrangements in the center of each table. A surprising number of glances were directed our way by diners, most of them older and white, couples and occasionally families of tow-headed blond children, but I at least was used to such attention. The host, who seemed to be either the owner or manager, was tall and dark haired and looked harried; he looked at our group for a long moment, walked behind a curtain, and returned a few minutes later to seat us in a back room walled off from the rest of the restaurant by two walls and two sets of curtains through which the serving staff entered and exited, and back there only one other couple, middle-aged and white, were in the room with us. We gossiped and joked about the previous weekend's festivities, during which a corps member named Nicholas Ware had done a number of keg-stands, something we hadn't seen since college, which seemed now ages ago.

Finally our server arrived at the table. She was young and blond, with long wavy Pantene-commercial hair that seemed popular with twenty-something white women in the Delta.

"Y'all will have to excuse me, it's my first night," she said in a deep Delta drawl. "Where are y'all from?"

As we answered, Portland, Eugene, Baltimore, Chicago, her face took on a grave expression, as if she had just received tragic news.

"Oh, my lord," she said gravely, her voice full of heartfelt sympathy. "Y'all must be them Teach America teachers. I am *so so* sorry y'all have to teach them monsters."

Flabbergasted at the assumptions implicit in her reaction, once she had left we lightened things up. Sarah, like Michael a first-year elementary school teacher, talked about how hard things were right now.

"This time last year," I commiserated, "I went to the highest building I could find and jumped out the window." I paused, grinned. "Being in this part of the Delta, it wasn't a fatal fall."

Tired and festive as we were, it struck us as particularly

funny, and we were laughing when the black busboy came to take the bread plates.

"May I take these?" he asked rather stiffly.

"Sure, go ahead," said Michael. His voice, which had been high and full with laughter, reverted to the low bass of his normal register. The busboy's face flushed.

"Lower your voice to me, will you?" he said threateningly. "Think you gone come to a place like this sitting with these all and lower your voice to me?"

There was a long tension during which we tried to explain that Michael's voice *was* low, and Michael apologized, and after a time the busboy stalked away. We sat a little dazed, wondering how exactly we had stepped over lines we weren't aware we were violating, not thinking about what it meant to sit two pretty young white women with a black man and an ambiguously brown fellow. Finally, I tried to lighten the mood.

"Well, look at us. A black man, a Chinaman, and two white women. It's like—multiculturalism comes to the Delta!"

Instead of the smiles I expected, the two girls looked horrified. I turned to find our waitress standing behind me with the water pitcher.

"Sooo," she said awkwardly, not meeting my eyes. "It'll just be another minute, y'all."

She retreated toward the kitchen while I winced. I was apologizing for the faux pas of talking about race when we heard a great crash and tinkle and clatter, then the sound of a host's angry voice.

"Great. You broke the whole order!"

"Shit," Michael said, keeping his voice to a whisper.

The rest of the night, as we waited for the order to be remade, we spoke only about safe topics like the weather and the topography of the Delta. The busboy did not return to our table. As we left, the host eyed Michael as if making a calculation, then pulled me aside and leaned down so he was whispering raspily in my ear. "Please don't y'all ever come back."

I looked him in the eye and said nothing, unwilling to acquiesce, but we never returned; we'd already committed to other battles bigger than we knew how to fight.

All year long, Michael and I had collaborated on units and resources; a much more naturally gifted educator than I was, he taught well from the beginning of his first year. Years later, he became the principal of a Delta school, and more recently the executive director of a Mississippi education nonprofit. We worked out a science unit, mostly by way of his impetus and labor, that included actual experiments and group work and scientific method and lab reports; my contribution was in writing, where all year I focused on description and writing sensory detail and organizing information in paragraphs, having students write autobiographies and describe their favorite game or the feel of the leather jacket I'd been gifted for college graduation from my family in Hawaii, and one day even bringing in an apple pie so that smell and taste could be the focus of an assignment.

"Oooweee, I'd write all the time if I had me some apple pie every day!" Solomon remarked slyly, knowing he'd elicit a smile.

The last unit was Michael's idea, and it was a great one: to have students do a research paper on the lives and achievements of great black Americans. The school library wasn't available, of course, as the children weren't allowed to check out nonfiction, but my own shelves sported a dozen biographies of sports stars and historically significant blacks, from Harriet Tubman to Jackie Robinson to George Washington

Carver, and we checked out all the books concerning famous black Americans from the Promise Public library, the librarian, an older white woman, eyeing us oddly but not remarking on our affinity for children's books concerning African Americans. The students were to take notes, compile and order and organize them, and finally go through the proofreading and revision process; in the end, the kids would type them out and we'd print them, and then each child would illustrate his or her paper with a color portrait, either in action or posed. We had to shuttle books between rooms, and some students had to share, which wasn't always successful, as there was one Michael Jordan book and three boys writing his story. But much of the process of teaching research and assembling the work went well even in the warming days of April, the children hurrying to the box to retrieve the books and spreading out their notebooks and scribbling furiously to get down this detail or that. Though she rarely sought my attention, one day Serenity's hand lifted from the corner, not waving but held high, and when I reached her she was beaming. She held open her book on Oprah, a celebrity she had insisted on writing about when I unearthed the book in a fifth-grade Teach For America classroom.

"Did you know, Mr. Copperman, that Oprah from Mississippi, too?"

I smiled and shook my head.

"And look how far she gone, how she become the most famous black woman in America. The book say she wouldn't never let nothing or nobody stop her."

As was usually the case with Serenity, I had nothing to say because she already got the point; I simply smiled and left her to go back to her book, throughout the room the only sound that of a shifting of beanbag chairs and the rustle of turned pages and the constant scritch of pencil to paper as the children took in lives of the sort I desperately wanted to believe they could have.

Each morning during those last months, I woke early to the throb of the alarm, the coffee to be made and shirt to be ironed and the whole imminent day of teaching ahead. Even so, I would take a moment to orient myself, to catch the sounds of birds and the distant rush of passing cars out the highway, the crackling shift of the heater if the pilot had lasted the night. For a few minutes I was only myself as I always have been, not Mr. Copperman of Room 12, not the fourth-grade teacher, but some guy named Mike who didn't know what he was doing, who'd never really known. And then the years that put me in this immediate life would recede to the necessity of what was ahead, the stakes of trying to offer what these children deserved in the time I had left. I did this morning after morning, something forcing me back before I could begin again—perhaps because in so many ways, I felt helpless to the magnitude of the task. That feeling receded only when I reached the school and found my kids at my door, when they rose from the ground and embraced me in the hall, calling "Mr. Copperman, good morning!" and continued to retreat as their voices bounded through the room clean with morning light, naming me who I was.

Teaching today at the university, every quarter I will examine course evaluations and find one from a student I failed to see, someone who felt that I ignored or disrespected them, a student who disliked me and seethed from a corner silently, unnoticed, even as I will also find a few students I have to strain to picture at all who quietly loved my class but had never asserted themselves in ways I'd noticed. So it was in the Delta, perhaps, and now, after a decade of memory's sifting and shuffling of chaff from jewel, I find the children who weren't loud or extraordinary emerging from memory to declare themselves. I picture the student named Tonka from my second year who was heavyset and freckled and perhaps not the brightest student, but who always followed every direction and who had such a thorough good nature, such a guileless and pleasing smile, that I used to compliment him just to see his freckled face break into a wide easy grin and bless us all with radiant goodwill. I picture Charleton, whom I mostly hated my first year because he was defiant and perpetually off task, telling me one recess to watch until I turned and gave him my full attention. He put his feet together, ran five loping paces, and quickly accelerated to a sudden sprint, turned a front handstand and a second and third and pivoted into a backflip that he landed with arms raised in a V like an Olympic gymnast. As I broke into applause, he met my gaze, winked, and bowed low, as if to say, well, that *was* pretty damn good, wasn't it?

I remember a boy named Medius who was hugely obese and socially awkward and who had to bind his khakis with two belts taped in the middle because his stomach was so large, the pants legs bunching and pooling at the ankles as they had been intended for a much taller child. He walked with such a sway of flesh side to side that if he stood to go to the bathroom or pick up a piece of paper or go to lunch he would often knock pencils and papers off other students' desks unless I sat him to the side and to the back. He would frequently act out for attention, stab his arm with staples so that they were stuck through the skin like a pierced hipster, glue his hands together so that he had to raise both in the air while the other students howled and I scowled. I remember how, during those rare moments when I spent time with him, keeping him perhaps on recess, which he preferred because other students would make fun of his size, he could be funny and silly and forget for a moment his plight at having been born into his own body, how he'd beam at a joke or compliment. I admit that too often I just wanted him and his antics to go away, that I cannot even recall now how he did on his end-of-year tests or even whose classroom he went on to in fifth grade, if he continued at all.

I recall a student named Letricia who had come originally from Chicago and who was at a loss in my chaotic classroom and whom I probably ignored over and over again trying to control and pacify and discipline the rest of the class. She had a delicate, gap-toothed smile and spoke sometimes with a slight lisp, which caused her quickly to stop talking at all after my mean girls mocked her despite my stern reprisal. She was devoutly Christian, believed in a way that most adults perhaps never truly do, with an absolute conviction that everything that happened could be ascribed to Jesus or to angels interceding in our lives. For a time, she used to put a note in my mailbox every day concerning what she called her "flight of angels."

She would write things like:

Dear Mr. Copperman, today my flight of angels come down and carried me on through when them kids was meddling me.

Today my flight of angels come down and told me my cousin in Memphis is in trouble and so I got my mama to call her mama and I talked to her and she said, "How'd you know?"

Today my flight of angels come and told me they was going help me learn my times tables all the way through twelve.

Today my flight of angels told me we all gone fly. Do you know to fly, Mr. Copperman?

I wish I could recall if I ever wrote her back or took her aside to thank her, but I was so frequently distracted by the moment-to-moment struggle for survival that too often I read the notes after they'd piled up, as I was hurrying to leave on a Friday afternoon, eager to finally go home. Halfway through the school year her mother abruptly moved her back to the Midwest. When I picture her now, I see only the beatific smile and the drawing that illustrated each note, of an angel carrying something like a harp or wand in outstretched arm, soaring off the page.

Marvin was another student whom I perhaps didn't notice enough at the time but whom I find myself thinking of often now. He was a slight, round-shouldered boy with a polite, halting manner and big, innocent brown eyes that seemed to take up his entire face. I must confess to having rarely paid him enough attention before I finally let Felicia Jackson fail—with her there, he was the sort of student who receded toward the background, easily lost in his own silence. He spoke softly, wanted badly to please; when praised he would blush and light up, then avert his head, unable to bear the scrutiny inherent in a compliment. He had less than most of his classmates—his uniform polos were moth eaten and his khakis stained and worn thin at the knees, and I gathered that, like so many Delta children, he lived with his mother and grandmother, and had no father in the picture.

Marvin's third-grade teacher had been another male Teach For America corps member whom he'd looked up to, and at the end of third grade Mr. Black had given Marvin a hardcover book that had been read aloud to the class but was grades above Marvin's independent reading level. Marvin wanted badly to read his book, which he carried around in his dog-eared backpack. Together, we set a goal that he'd read the book by the end of the year. He didn't want to wait, would take out the book during readers' workshop and battle his way, syllable by syllable, through the compound words he couldn't yet decode, an activity so frustrating he'd clench his fists and shake. Finally, I made him promise to stop reading it for a while so that he could see his own improvement. Marvin begrudgingly agreed, though each day he'd take out the book and set it before him as a reminder of his goal.

He waited a solid month before picking the book back up; the first time through, it took him nearly a month. I would wince when I saw him struggling word by word during reading time, his brow furrowed, his mouth soundlessly forming words. Yet he wouldn't choose another book, and he was comprehending what he was reading through sheer, dogged force of will. When he finally finished, he opened the book back to the first page and started again; the second time it took him two weeks, the third time a week. After five cycles I finally got him to move to the second book in the Boxcar series, and soon enough he was able to lay claim to all thirty Boxcar books on my shelves. I made him our official "Boxcar Specialist," and he guided other students through tours of the series, giving plot summaries and recommendations.

Every day Marvin would stay with me after school, cleaning the room, discussing his latest Boxcar book, or surfing the Internet on the computer. His goal was to last until it got dark so that I would give him a ride home in my "wagon"— he liked nothing better than to be rolling through the pot-holed streets riding shotgun, Nas bumping from the speakers

(*I know I can / Be what I wanna be / If I work hard at it / I'll be where I wanna be*), arm trailing out the window to touch the passing air.

There were some "bumps" with Marvin. The worst of it was during the three-week period when his mom let his medication lapse, a nightmare of temper tantrums and reckless hyperactivity. His concentration span shrank to next to nothing, and his self-control was gone. I wrote note after note home and once even sent Marvin to the office after he tried to punch Solomon for stepping on his jacket at recess, but nothing worked. The medication was expensive, his mother told me, and besides, Marvin didn't *really* need it. Soon Marvin couldn't sleep at night, and with constant insomnia, he took to calling me late, dialing me at midnight and past.

"What's going on?" I asked groggily.

"I got so much to do," he'd mumble vaguely. "But I don't know what. Or where I am. Where am I?"

I was at a loss; I thought about offering to fill the prescription myself, whatever the liability. Then one Monday Marvin came back to school with a huge white bandage on his hand and a whole new attitude. You could see the difference in his body language and demeanor.

"What happened to you?" I asked.

"I punched out the window," he said happily. In a fit of rage over something inconsequential, Marvin had put his hand through a plate-glass window, cutting himself badly. The emergency room doctor had refused to take the explanation of "accident" and, having gotten to the bottom of the thing, had insisted that the prescription be refilled. I wasn't happy with what it had taken, but I was nonetheless thankful to have the old Marvin back in my classroom.

In late spring, Delta Horizons, the Title I program that I taught aikido in after school, organized a trip to Washington,

DC. Marvin was a part of the program. We'd come up with full funding—all the children had to do was get a permission slip signed. Marvin kept shrugging when I asked him about the slip, and so I told him of the wide green lawns and sparkling reflective pools, the great columns and towers, all the history and grandeur he'd witness, and he promised to get the slip signed. When he did, I didn't request the fifty dollars of meal money that was required; I put in the money from my own pocket.

That April, on the two-day bus ride to DC, through the furrowed fields and dusty flats of Tennessee, then threading the rolling green hills of Virginia, Marvin reread his book. I watched him there, holding the pages to the window as the landscape flashed past in blocks of green and brown, reading the words aloud, laughing sometimes to himself with delight at the familiar turns and twists, sometimes racing for me along the aisle as other chaperones called for him to finally sit down, eager to tell me everything that had just happened.

On the great green lawn of the Capitol Building, Marvin stood delighted less by the spectacle of Capitol Hill than by the book he held victoriously in hand, the glory of his own achievement: he'd finished, and he'd come a long way indeed.

As we neared the end of the year, the pressure to realize final results mounted for those of us who were Teach For America corps members. I reluctantly participated in the push to do well on the Mississippi Curriculum Test, the nation- and state- and district- and school-wide mandate to reach 100 percent proficiency in math, reading, and writing. We had rallies and visits from state officials and reverends who insisted that God would bless the test if the children kept Jesus in their hearts. We were told to dedicate an hour each afternoon to test-taking practice and strategy, and we were forced to administer mock Mississippi Curriculum Tests and assess our results and compare them; I refused to teach the test-taking strategy but had no choice but to give the children the mock tests. "Man, shoot," Solomon exclaimed at recess after a morning dedicated to taking the full-length MCT practice test. "Seem like we got to take a lot of tests just to take a test. Can't we just do it once?"

I smiled, wished I could agree out loud; yet I was afraid of what the children might repeat about how Mr. Copperman didn't care about the tests and didn't make them go to computers to practice. Today, years after George W. Bush administration officials admitted that No Child Left Behind was a failure, as the Barack Obama administration is in the late stages of deconstructing the dysfunctional policies that lingered in its aftermath, it seems obvious that such an extreme focus on testing and the practice of "motivating" administrators and teachers with the threat of punishment was wrongheaded and ineffective. On the ground in those early years, we were told that a refusal to buy in fully reflected either our own lack of professionalism or a lack of faith in our students' capacity to achieve despite their poverty and our school's lack of resources. I kept my mouth shut, but it was a tremendous relief when the three days of testing were finally done; a weight seemed to lift from the entire school.

For those of us in Teach For America frantic to meet our personal, programmatic goals, however, pressure persisted. I was using a computer program to test reading level, a practice that now sounds absurdly imprecise, and a math diagnostic that was almost certainly not adequately varied or rigorous. Even so, as the results began to come in, I charted them frantically, aggregating and averaging, trying to figure out if I had in fact "reached my big goal of significant achievement." "Significant achievement," what a phrase—the idea that the focus was on what a teacher had done, that numbers on a page had any real relation to the long-term impact of such service. One late April afternoon during readers' workshop, which had mounted now to fifty-seven unbroken minutes of full-class focused reading, I found that the final numbers had come out all right, that I had indeed "achieved significant gains." I stood, felt a flush of joy and pride, and almost broke the silence and ended our month-long string of days increasing by at least a minute. I looked about the class, afternoon sunlight gold through the window throwing hot white blocks of light to the floor and reading rug and striking a silvery shimmer off the glitter I'd let the children use on the borders of their mounted biographies of famous African Americans. Solomon, who was flat on his stomach with his feet dangling beneath my desk, glanced at me standing over him and then quickly returned his eyes to his book, while Marvin remained engrossed in his book beside him, their knees touching, reading each word in an almost audible whisper. I could see only Serenity's head and the top of her book visible from behind the big blue beanbag in the corner; Demichael wrote a careful note in his book log with a smile on his face, another book finished and recorded and done with his tendency, which I'd fought all year, to value volume of books read over the books' reading level, before he shuffled through his book basket for the next one. Looking at them, I let the easy sentiment wash over me: We did this together! And then, before I could even enjoy it, immediately the first pang of loss seized me: soon, I would leave, and I might never see these children again. I set the paper with its scores and statistics face down on my desk and left it there to resume book-log conferences with the kids, knowing already how little such numbers mattered.

The last day of school was difficult. Our end-of-the-year slide show, shown to whooping applause in the final minutes, had us all tearing up. Marvin was especially inconsolable, huddled at the back corner for much of the afternoon. I tried to talk to him, but his stricken face was beyond consolation.

"Why do all my teachers go away?" he finally said.

"Yeah, Mr. C. Why you gone go on and leave us? Is it cause you don't like us?" Solomon piped up.

I looked around the classroom, and agreement and accusation was there on Serenity's face, and Deshawn's; Precious was nodding, too. I felt my throat seize; I didn't have an explanation.

"I've told Willie all about our class, and he wants you when he's in fourth grade," said Serenity.

"My little brother, too!" Precious said.

"Who'll teach us aikido next year in Delta Horizons?" asked Marvin.

I turned my palms up as if the answer was in them.

"Just tell me the truth, Mr. Copperman," Solomon said, his usual joking voice turned serious. "Is it that you have to leave? Or do you just want to leave?"

I turned away as my eyes teared up. Was I abandoning them? My place wasn't in the Delta. But how do you explain to a ten-year-old that you must leave him behind?

I didn't explain, except to tell the kids that it wasn't them; even now, I can't answer.

AFTERMATH

RETURNS

It didn't happen often, white as Oregon is, until the summer I taught a class up Interstate 5 in an attempt to get to the city and away from my life. When my department chair offered the class, apologizing for the hassle of travel, I signed on eagerly and found a sublet in a couple's house out M. L. K. Boulevard in North Portland at the edge of Alberta, a neighborhood that was gentrifying more by the day, the old brick houses and empty shops on the main drag getting paint and false fronts, becoming kitschy shops and swanky bars where hipsters congregated in tight-jeaned packs. The Terrell Brandon barber shop and the beauty supply and the corner market, old businesses that had survived and still filled up with black customers from the neighborhood during the day, stood dark and silent at night as the bars filled with hipsters howling bohemian cries of joy and riot. Each morning I woke early and walked out into the neighborhood, away from commerce and out toward the parks and projects: one-story brick houses and white ranchos with wide porches and yellowing lawns and chain-link fences and music from inside dim rooms that was only a throb of base, and the black people who lived there out in the new summer light, old folks on easy chairs on porches and swings and rockers, young men on corners bumping shoulders and clasping hands, boys calling out over the echo of ball to concrete playing pick-up on hoops in cul-de-sacs and corner lots, women calling to one another across streets, girls playing hopscotch, families walking hand in hand with young children, mothers calling out to little ones lagging behind, *Get up here, baby! Come on now*. Children seized by the hand, admonished gently with explanation, *Got to keep you safe.*

I'd walk block after block, taking in the sights, feet crunching the occasional gravel and staying mostly to the sidewalk, walking the edges of Rosa Parks and Peninsula and Farrington Park with the shade of their great old trees and children running in the grass, turning from the whoosh and thrum of the freeway as I neared, going down only as far as the overlook over the train tracks and the great green fairway beyond. Drinking it in, thirsty for the familiar cadence of voices, for the sound of children crowing, cajoling, chortling, howling with delight, talking big, talking back. Feeling for a moment the years retreat; feeling for a moment that I'd gone back a decade, was again on the streets of Promise. And sometimes, when I'd walked long enough and the sun was at an even height throwing short, sharp shadows and I had forgotten myself adequately, I'd think I saw them in a crowd waiting at a crosswalk, or in a group outside an arcade or convenience store: a girl's head held high and proud, a boy clowning with windmilling arms, the shadow of a child's cornrowed head and mischief in a flash of eyes. I'd stop and stare, blinking my eyes, trying to be sure. Thinking somehow it was my kids here and now, that I could still return to them.

This is all there is, the world tells Delta kids. These razor-wire fences to keep you out or in, these cinder-block walls and ill-lit halls, and all these doors to dead-end rooms. Here are the streets dusty and blank, this queue of tin-roofed shacks, the bowing boards of porches, these sun-scorched flats and this ragged edge of cotton field that you can't claim, you can't sow or reap—you can't. I came and declared, "You can!," said it again and again hoping each time that it would sound less hollow.

The Delta changed me. People speak of how idealism ought to be tempered by experience and think that it's a benign process: growing older, becoming wiser. They're wrong. You can't restore faith. I wouldn't have been teaching a decade now at the University of Oregon if it weren't for those two years in the Delta, would long ago have traded in my Stanford degree for a job with status and decent pay. Each day in the classroom with eighteen-year-olds of diverse background, I see my fourth graders grown up, and a part of me imagines that somehow I am speaking directly to the children for whom I wanted so much. Yet back in Promise, children I taught walk the dusty streets headed nowhere, and I don't have it in me to help them. It isn't work ethic I lack, but the courage to fail—to fail again to save a child who doesn't have a fighting chance.

Some nights I lie awake bargaining, trying to get back to the man I was, and imagine choices: if I could trade my comfortable life for theirs, if I could take their lot and free them from poverty, would I? So simple to say, *of course*, when there are guarantees.

I dream of carrying children to safety from fires, of bearing them across ravines in a storm, of leading the way through a dark wood and a line of children behind following blindly, grudgingly, until we emerge in a city with clean, bright streets, the very air shimmering with possibility, and they are with me despite all our doubts. We've arrived.

When I wake, the relief is bitterly lost: I am alone in my high-rise apartment with all the comforts of a middle-class life, and those children are a world away in shacks on the wrong side of the tracks, hearing the bark of a stray dog, the far-off whistle of the train bound elsewhere, always elsewhere. I left them behind, and so cannot let go.

In late fall in the Willamette Valley, the rain-darkened streets narrow. The trees bow over leaf-covered sidewalks, bare branches silhouetted against a bone-white sky. I drive slowly with the heater on high, the flat light failing against tinted windows, and in the browning fallen leaves, the chill that comes through glass, I see the long winter ahead and am thankful there is still work at the university: papers to grade, students who demand response and energy before I'm done. Necessity. I've often felt, since that trip back to the Delta, that I do not know what I am doing—for years, I've told myself that now I teach in a position where I can make a difference, that here in Eugene, Oregon, teaching young adults to think critically and communicate, I make a difference. Returning to Promise, I saw the thinness of that claim—how the little I thought I'd done right came to nothing, how teaching now is only a futile attempt to make good on promises I long ago failed to keep. Often, it feels as if even my best efforts in the classroom are doomed to failure.

One fall quarter a couple of years ago, I began class with the syllabus, went through roll, and made my usual joke about calling students by the names they wanted to go by: "If you say you want to go by G-Money, I *will* call you G-Money for the rest of the quarter!"

I went about the room of faces of every hue and color taking names, Thuc and Tarik and Donte, Roselily, Mercedes, Angelique who went by Angel, and Patric-ia who went by Trish. This writing class was perhaps my fiftieth teaching low-income, first-generation minority students at the university, and I proceeded with the assurance of experience. I came to a tall, thin, dark-skinned young black man in baggy jeans and a backward basketball cap, who said nothing when it came his turn, just stared for a long and uncomfortable silence, grinned in a flash of startlingly white teeth, then said, "Bad."

I glanced at my roll, at a name that was long and perhaps Muslim or African. "You want to go by 'Bad'?"

He glanced at his classmates, gave a sly nod in my direction as if to make it clear that he and they were in on the shared assessment that this teacher was a ridiculous square, that his tyranny had to be fought with subversion. "I *am* Bad," he said with a wink, and the class laughed nervously, and I moved on. Later, as I bantered with another girl in class, the young man said something that elicited a stir from the students near him, and when I glanced over he met my gaze and held it with an unsettling intensity. I decided not to call him "Bad," to call him by his listed name, Caron. I made a mental note to try to connect with him, to demonstrate that I cared about where he came from and what he cared about— to show him that I was on his side.

Over the ensuing weeks, it became clear that Caron had no intention of accepting my overtures or respecting my authority. He followed overt instructions begrudgingly, with an exaggerated slowness, moving to a group only after everyone else had already gone so as to make clear how burdensome the instructions were, opening his book only if asked a second time, crossing his arms and slouching down in his chair with hat brim tipped low if he was asked to discuss with others. Then, during group discussion, he began to assert himself covertly: each time I spoke, asking a question or making a comment, he averted his face from view and began to speak in a low voice, mockingly lilting in imitation of my tone and cadence, eliciting a murmur of reaction from nearby students. I tried to ignore it, but soon all I could focus on was the voice and its indistinct, hostile invocations; I felt again that uneasy, sickly dread of being in a classroom where things were wrong, and bad ends imminent. I called Caron over one day after class. "I'd appreciate it if you'd stop speaking when I am. It's disrespectful."

He raised his eyebrows, grinned with a flash of teeth. "I'm not speaking while you are."

I stood, mute in the face of his blatant denial, and finally walked away. Yet there was no walking away from the persistent distraction and the ways it derailed the progress of the class and poisoned its culture, how it silenced other students wary of contributing under conditions where everything offered was reflexively scorned. A single student, no matter how worthy or challenged, should not be allowed to harm others' educational experience—that was the lesson of Felicia Jackson, after all—and I felt I'd learned nothing, could again do nothing. I called my favorite counselor from the office charged with supporting at-risk students, and I spoke to a woman who often worked wonders with her students; she reported that he remained closed to her, that he wouldn't say anything, just sat with arms crossed watching her with what she called the "stink-eye." All she could tell me was that he was a first-generation African immigrant from a poor neighborhood and rough high school and that he was doing poorly in all his classes so far. She promised to talk to him, but nothing changed.

Each day I had to teach, a knot in my stomach began to form hours before class began, a queasy sinking. Mississippi had taught me that there was no reprieve in the refrain *What's the worst thing that could happen?*; the consequence of defiance like Caron's was chaos, trauma, and failure. I'd thought that this job, teaching these deserving, unprivileged students, was redemption—that I'd become a better teacher and a better man. Now doubt came flooding back.

I tried to understand, spoke to Caron after class and in meetings in my office during which he crossed his arms and smiled at me with what seemed to me to be a leer, sneering and implacable, as he said again and again that he would stop doing "whatever I claimed he was." His denial was as infuriating as my efforts were ineffectual; I was far past the point where the problem was with my effort or innovation or compassion. Not all students can be reached, whatever platitudes about educational justice and good teaching I preferred to declare; to let Caron derail the class further was to betray the rest of the students.

I went to the director of composition, explained to her the extraordinary circumstances, and begged her for an extraordinary accommodation for the remaining weeks of the quarter, during which the class was writing an essay about their personal identity: I'd work with Caron one-on-one by email, and accept his work and grade it, but he would no longer attend class and so disrupt it.

I could easily have failed him, though his work itself was competent; I could have had a case with student conduct that well might have ended his undergraduate career or at least have marred his transcript, and surely he didn't deserve my generosity. But in a half-decade of teaching children raised from poverty, one salient observation recurred so often that I refused to ignore it: there are reasons why people act as they do. Not excuses, but reasons so deep as to render my assumptions and reactions inevitably inadequate.

I knew I was missing something, but it was sweet relief to walk into that composition class without Caron there and feel that knot of dread unwind; the sound of those students' voices without the undercurrent of threat was a beautiful clamor of eager engagement. All was not lost—a kid from that class whom I paid far less attention to than I would have liked, a Persian American kid named Harpo, who hailed from inner-city Oakland and who wore a flat-brimmed Raiders cap at a forty-five-degree angle, became so animated in trying to describe to clueless me what Hyphy music was as a lifestyle and identity that he stood in the middle of class to demonstrate what it meant to "go dumb." I can tell you that Harpo told me last year, at a graduation ceremony for scholars of diverse background, that what carried him through rough patches of his undergraduate career was what I said the first day of class before Caron asserted himself as being "Bad": "This class is challenging and demanding, but you all belong here at the university and deserve your place in this class. Work hard, and I promise you will succeed."

And here is what little I can tell you about why Caron felt he had to be "Bad": first, that he himself didn't know. He wrote in his identity essay that he was lost being at the university, insecure with his intellectual ability and capacity, and terrified of failing his family and their hopes and dreams, and that acting out against authority was the way he'd gotten through high school, where he never felt he belonged as an African immigrant in a historically black and poor area. That he had tried and tried to stop, but found his mouth opening each time I spoke as if by its own accord; that he hadn't been offering satire or commentary but simply been repeating my words verbatim, which the students around him had not been delighted with but had resented and thought idiotic, so that the sounds I'd heard were often them begging him to be quiet. That he was ashamed. That he'd been ashamed his entire life, of being himself, of being exposed, and of who he'd been—that he'd felt that way since he was a child back in Africa, and militia soldiers had come looking for his brother and father, and had dragged him out from the table where he'd been hiding, and placed the rifle barrel to his temple and made him tell them where his mother was hiding, where his father and brother might be, that in his fear he would have betrayed everything he loved and so he trusted himself least of all. That he was sorry, and thankful for the second chance, and that though I shouldn't forgive him for how he'd been, he'd make no excuses from here on out.

I saw Caron across the room at the same graduation ceremony where I spoke to Harpo. Perhaps I was staring, and Caron felt my gaze; he turned in his seat, and our eyes met and recognition flashed across his face. He didn't smile, but he didn't look away, just met my gaze and then nodded once, slowly, as if to affirm that he'd kept his word, and there was nothing else now between us.

VOICES

I sat in a high-ceilinged, murmurous lecture hall, half-full with Oregon sociology professors and grad students and interested members of the public, watching Stanford sociologist Doug Osterhout configure his Powerpoint presentation and banter with colleagues and grad students who stood about him in an admiring pack. He was a tall, wiry, tanned fellow who carried himself with the casual assurance of a Stanford professor who'd long ago arrived. I knew the type well—I'd perhaps been on a path to becoming so confident and successful a fellow before Teach For America, though now when I speak of Stanford I find myself saying that it was so lovely and idyllic a place as to ruin you permanently for the rest of the world.

In the rear, someone dimmed the lights a little; Osterhout fired up the projector, cleared his throat into the mic, and then gave a broad grin and crossed his arms about his chest and said, "Hello, now, University of Oregon! If you don't mind, let's begin with some background about Teach For America."

Osterhout's presentation was efficient enough in defining educational inequality and Teach For America's operational mission. Then he shifted into his own research concerning the long-term impact of Teach For America on the character of its corps members. He was known for his study of the long-term effects of the three-month 1968 Mississippi Freedom Summer on the character and civic commitment of volunteers. That research found that those volunteers were deeply radicalized by their experiences in Mississippi during that turbulent time. This work, forthcoming in his latest book, contrasted how Freedom Summer participants became engaged in the political movements of the time with the ways that Teach For America alums prove less engaged in long-term civic commitment, service, and philanthropy. I was well aware of this conclusion—Osterhout had already gone national with his conclusions in a number of Associated Press and *New York Times* articles with titles like "Teach For America Makes Bad Citizens." As a Teach For America alum, I was understandably interested in hearing the justification for his conclusions.

Osterhout's work on the Mississippi Freedom Summer seemed clear and vigorous—he'd been able to find all the original applications and conduct extensive follow-up interviews with both those individuals who hadn't gone to Mississippi that summer and those who had, and he'd found that people and the course of their lives were deeply affected, that many of the volunteers had turned toward political activism, given the rabid opposition they faced and in some cases the attendant danger—volunteers were lynched that summer, and some were threatened by racist mobs. In conducting the interviews, Osterhout said, he'd come to understand just how deeply the violence and intensity of that summer had altered those volunteers, how afterward they couldn't return to the lives they'd left because they'd been changed.

Then, Osterhout shifted to his work with Teach For America. "Here with Teach For America, what you find is exactly the opposite," he said.

I felt the blood rise to my face—was he really saying that there had been no intensity to the Teach For America experience? According to statistical analysis, Teach For America alums, while good citizens by any "normal" standard, didn't participate in American civic life at as high a rate as people who had either declined to join when offered a chance or who had dropped out during their term of service. Finally, he said, it wasn't difficult to explain why the character of Mississippi Freedom Summer volunteers had been improved, while Teach For America corps members were unaffected.

He clicked Powerpoint forward. On the screen, the slide said in bold letters:

**Freedom Summer participants experienced
real trauma.
Teach For America corps members only taught**.

I stared at the slide until the letters blurred, found that I was shaking with disbelief. Only taught? I clutched the arms of my chair, holding in a critique savaging the shallowness of the research, how it was foolish to trust regressions on data gleaned from a survey that itself had a less than 50 percent return rate, protesting that if Osterhout hadn't conducted follow-up interviews or other ethnography to try to find out about corps members' experiences and subsequent choices then he'd found out nothing, that he shouldn't speculate about people he didn't even know. I let every objection run through my brain until the rage subsided a little, until I knew I could be reasonable. I waited for the question-and-answer period, raised my hand and waited my turn, and stood and spoke before the hostile crowd.

"My name is Michael Copperman," I said. "I teach low-income, first-generation, at-risk students of color here at the UO in an effort to retain them. I taught fourth grade in the rural black public schools of the Mississippi Delta with Teach For America from 2002 to 2004. And quite respectfully, I think you've got it wrong."

I told the crowd that the people I knew from Teach For America in the Delta had largely stayed in education, that of the people I was still in touch with, one was now a teacher in a low-income area of Portland, one worked still for Teach For America sixty and seventy hours a week, one was the vice president of a large national education nonprofit, another had been a school principal in the Delta and now was the executive director of an education nonprofit, and three more were still directly fighting against educational inequality, myself included, most of us working for a fraction of the salaries we could be making in the private sector. I noted that the reason ethnographic methods are available to the sociologist is precisely because the explanatory power of numbers is necessarily limited, that without follow-up interviews Osterhout had no idea just how affecting the Teach For America experience was, that he couldn't imagine what it was like to be in America's most troubled schools, to be responsible for children with so much promise and so little opportunity. Finally, Osterhout, who had craned his head a little to the side as if to suggest the questionable nature of my assertions, interrupted me.

"Listen," he said, in a tone that conveyed pity for the unreasoned passion of my objections, "you're never going to believe the truth. You will always trust your experiences rather than hard, rigorous facts—you're hopelessly subjective. Please sit down, and be quiet."

I began to object, felt the eyes of the room judging me, begging that I remain silent; I felt the burden of conveying all that hadn't been said, of somehow making this man and this room and the entire world see the children I taught, and how much they deserved, felt all their voices rise up in my throat and assail me as I nodded and sat, not knowing where to start, what else to say. And as Osterhout cracked a joke and the crowd laughed, somewhere in my subconscious a less rhetorical accusation arose, not an indictment of this research or its questionable conclusions but a deeper and uglier stirring, something like recognition or guilt: what had Teach For America done to me? Had it indeed made me a worse person? Why did I so often think of the experience with trepidation, flinching from events I couldn't face; why did I still feel such guilt at having left the Delta to go on with my life? Why did I so often feel that I was not all right at all?

On the way home after hearing Osterhout speak, heavy fog clung to the road, and I drove half-blind and trusted in NPR. There was talk of the endlessly ongoing war, troop increases and persistent violence, of swine flu and salmonella in peanut butter. It was slow going until the fog broke at Junction City. In the rearview mirror, solid white, and ahead the flat grass-seed fields with their early spring stubble, hills bunched on the horizon. The falling sun cast shadows behind each car, each passed tree. And on the radio, a story of a charter in the Bronx. An arts school for the underprivileged, demographics meaning black, straining not to say it, to couch it in statistics, implied and therefore understood. A teacher, a white voice, spoke of student achievement. A little black girl's voice, self-important, hopping with the cadence of poverty: "Them teacher just come up in here and show us all kind thing. Teach us some dance. Got camera and computer and paint. Make me want to learn."

I almost saw her: hair in tight fresh braids, hands clasped behind her back, and head canted in question: Do you hear me telling you what you want to hear? And in a moment, a clamor of voices tumbled over each other with urgency and innocence, poise and precipice, need. Though I was three thousand miles from a life I had left, I was elsewhere again. I turned off the radio and let the vibration of the road be the only sound, let myself return to the Delta, to how I was, who I was, when I believed I could save a child:

"C'mon and pitch it, Mr. C! Hey now! How you gone do me like that? That don't count as no strike!"

"But I got to USE—I got to use, to use, to, what all you call it, Mr. Copperman, I got to 'pee'—or I gone do myself right here!"

"What the capital of Ory-gun in is, Mr. Copperman? Everybody live in a tree out there, right?"

"Mr. Copperman, I'm gone tell you God's own truthfullest truth. Last night I was finishing the math homework and mama told me to go to bed, and I said, 'But mama, I got to do this here for my man-teacher cause I want to have a good future and go on to college and become president,' and mama said, 'Boy, your future is I'm gone wear your black butt out if you don't go to bed,' and she just shake her head and go on like she fitting to go for her switch, and mama swing one **mean** switch, and so you see, it was mama's fault I didn't finish that homework for you!"

"How come you always got to talk so careful, Mr. C, all like, 'Hello, my children, today is a day when we speak using all the words we have in our dictionary here'?"

"Mr. Copperman, how come you not black and you not white but you say you like Nas? Don't you got some Asian person music or something so you ain't stealing folks' music?"

"But Mr. Copperman, how you know if you don't like a Kool-Aid pickle if you ain't had none?"

"Oooowee, look at he face—he don't like them pickles!"

"Mr. Copperman, this a poem I wrote for you. Roses are red, Violets is blue, You making a face like you stepped in poo."

"Man, shoot. That ain't nothing. That like half a poem. Here a real poem: "Roses is dead. And violets dead too. Cause I on fire, and this —— just burned you."

"That ain't no poem—you can't use no swear words in no poem."

"Mr. Copperman, is that a poem?"

"Mr. Copperman! Mr. Copperman! Mr. Copperman!"

And they are with me again, clamoring to be heard, eyes bright, cheeks shiny, hair shaved close on the boys or braided to tight rows or pulled back clean in buns on the girls, their uniform polos starched and their khakis belted tight, sitting straight in "listening learning position" or slouching beneath their desks with arms crossed or buried in a beanbag chair or crouched deep in a kicker's stance at the plate on the kickball field or speaking while doing the heel-toe two-step at a sock hop beneath the strobing lights, arms and hands waving, faces upraised, demanding my attention in calling out, joking, declaiming, being absurd and serious and smart and so full of joy and anger and outrage and curiosity, such—kids.

And so it is: the further I am from the Delta, the clearer I hear them—perhaps this nearness in distance is how the past clarifies as it recedes from reach, so that finally what is left is distilled, too perfect to bear. Those kids are after all no longer children but full-grown men and women who likely even have children of their own and jobs and aspirations and adult burdens now. They are no longer my charge, but they are with me as they were: faces bright, voices loud. And because what happened then is inalterable, it is possible now to love them purely as they were, without the need to have them behave or achieve.

Perhaps that is why I have begun to forgive myself for having failed them—because maybe I didn't fail them after all, any more than they failed me. They were smart, good kids, beautiful in all they didn't know and all they wanted. The poverty that limited them could be ugly, but they were not.

And while I could be ugly in my frustration and all the arrogant naïveté of youth, I was not such a bad teacher. Not as good as they deserved, but as good a teacher under the circumstances as I could manage. There was nothing wrong with me or wrong with them. We were a classroom, and for a time a sort of family.

Though there was so much trauma and trouble and loss along the way that for a decade I couldn't understand why I kept gazing back, mulling over what was gone, it finally is simple: I left a part of my heart in the Delta. Since I left, I've always held back a little, unwilling to risk everything again the way I did back when I didn't know you couldn't change the world through force of will. A part of me will always remain with those kids, and I will always yearn to return to them, to be with them once more and hear the cadence of their voices, see their upturned, eager faces, and have time for just one more chapter read aloud, one more times table and one more lesson, one last chance to be there with them and so be whole again—to be once more, simply and only, *teacher*.

I arrive at my office one morning like any other fall morning, hours to prepare before I teach and the usual papers to grade, copies to make. The morning is cool but not wet, but it is too warm inside the office building, and I find I can't concentrate on the grading, finally let myself check my email. The usual spam that's past the filters, students saying they are ill and asking questions, and I write cursory answers. Then I am surprised to see an email from Mr. Black, who'd taught some of the same kids I had in Mississippi. He sends greetings, is a lawyer in Birmingham now. He's read something I wrote about teaching in the Delta recently in a magazine that moved him, and thought I'd want to see "this." Attached is a PDF of an article from the town newspaper in Rosewood. They've published lists of the honors students from all the local high schools, including Promise; kids we taught are on the list. I look at the highest honor: Principal's List for Straight As. There are only four names, and at the top of tenth grade is Serenity Warner.

For a couple of days, I tell everyone who will listen about what I've found, how there can't be two Serenity Warners—surely not, it has to be her, right? A friend suggests that I Google her; it occurs to me that I am not the brightest citizen of the twenty-first century if someone else has to make this suggestion. I find a MySpace profile, a young woman from Promise with Serenity's features, her high, round forehead and soft chin, her wide smile. I set up an account and email her, tell her how proud I am of her making the list, tell her how I saw the house and was so worried about what had happened.

A day later comes a reply. There is a new profile photo, and the young woman is unmistakably Serenity. She is beaming, her cheeks round and shiny, her face round with health; her hair is pulled back neatly into a bun. My hand shakes as I open the message:

"Mr. Copperman, so good to hear from you!!!"

She's doing great, explains that after the fire, the state stepped in, that for the past four or five years she's been living with her adopted mother and father, actually her grandparents on a side she hadn't had much contact with back when she was with her mother. She says she's happy and loved, that her brother Willie is doing all right, that her senior year is on its way and that she's going to keep getting good grades so her future is ensured. She says she still loves to read.

I picture Serenity now, this grown young woman in the

picture with so much warmth in her smile, gazing down at a book perched on a counter in a clean kitchen bright with afternoon light.

She is all right after all—and so perhaps I am all right after all.

Finally, though I am no cheerleader for Teach For America, I can't agree with the organization's detractors. And I must admit that the substance of my defense is, with all apologies to Doug Osterhout, indeed hopelessly subjective. During my time in the Delta, we were constantly bombarded with messages about what we must achieve as Teach For America corps members: *You* must have big goals for your students. *You* must achieve significant gains. *You* must close the achievement gap, must work hard enough and effectively enough that your children succeed. These directives were compelling to elite overachievers, exemplars of the "me" generation who all believed themselves infinite in potential. The bitter limits of what a naïve, inexperienced teacher can manage in our nation's most troubled public schools, the recognition of one's own inadequacies, runs some 10 percent of Teach For America teachers from the classroom within a year; I suspect that two years of enduring disappointment, of feeling like a failure given the gulf between expectation and actual achievement, accounts for the lower levels of civic participation among Teach For America alums. Teach For America's cause is so just that the devotion it demands may finally be, for many corps members, too much responsibility to bear. Find an easier calling, return to the path toward success you were on in the kinder and more reasonable rest of the world where your abilities and talents are celebrated. Who can begrudge that choice?

The merit of Teach For America is not definable in a line

of argumentation or logic; it can't be found in a regression of numbers or a new study's conclusions concerning testable outcomes. Teach For America's merit is that it bridges the gap between worlds: a product of Princeton comes to a middle school in the Rio Grande Valley, the valedictorian of New York University ends up in inner-city Phoenix, and a fresh-faced kid from Stanford faces a classroom full of fourth graders who are more than his match. That contact creates a seam in the social fabric of the country—one that may well not hold, but not an insignificant bond nonetheless. Teaching alters the teacher as much as the student; the ways the children changed me were greater than my impact was on them. Today, I also sustain the hope that, like Serenity Warner, some children can rise from the ashes, not *because* of my teaching but perhaps not entirely despite it. Regardless, I will always carry their stories and voices; they have become a part of who I am. My commitment today to working with first-generation, low-income students of diverse background, then, is finally personal: I have a deep need, given what I saw in the Delta, to offer students what little I can. My students drop out of the university at two to three times the rate of majority students; I am part of a modest effort to retain them. Sometimes, too often, it is not enough, but that is often about the lack of mutuality in the exchange: students don't invest enough to succeed, or bear a history that makes the university the wrong place for them right now. Still, in a college classroom, teaching eighteen-year-olds writing, I am a better teacher than I was at twenty-two teaching fourth grade. Consider another student I taught in the fall and spring a couple of years ago—let's call her Leticiana Philips. Leticiana was about six feet tall, a lanky, young black woman who seemed all knees and elbows, except for a proud, sharp chin. She favored gold bracelets and chains and hoop ear-

rings, so that a musical jangling announced her every movement. She pulled her cornrows back high and tight, which
gave her a long brow and a look of composure and calm—until she spoke. That was when it came, the rush of words, elo-
quently nonstandard, chaotically staccato, at once assertive
and urgent and unconsidered. The first day, for example, her
arm shot to the ceiling in response to my suggestion that my
students call me "Mike":

"What this is bout calling somebody who teach at the University of Oregon some Mr. Mike or what-all ever? That ain't
respectful or right and don't make no sense. I'm just gone call
you teacher. *Teacher*."

I spluttered out something like yes.

It wasn't that Leticiana was unaccomplished—she was
at the university on a scholarship, former valedictorian of
Washington High, among the poorest schools in Portland.
I admit to seeing much of Felicia Jackson in Leticiana—as if
perhaps Leticiana were who Felicia Jackson might have become if she'd been dealt a slightly better hand. Yet Leticiana
had had a lot of "white teacher's help," as she put it, with
the essays that had gotten her into the university. And she
was, overall, a bit—unpolished—for college. Not to mention unrestrained. The day we discussed an essay about Native American mascots and team names, she stood up in the
middle of the discussion and interrupted me midsentence to
declare:

"Stop! Teacher, stop! Now all y'all listen." She went on to
explain that we didn't know a thing about being Indian. She
was half Cherokee on her mother's side and had stayed a
summer with her uncle out on the reservation. And did we
have any idea what it was like in a place in the middle of nowhere with some ugly little trees, a bathtub standing in a dirt
yard by a rusted-out pickup truck, and a house half-falling

down, walls bowing toward the middle and a tin roof with holes? Did we know why her uncle had a bumper sticker saying, "If you're Indian, you're in trouble," and did we understand that conditions were just like the author said: everybody drinking and drinking because there was nothing else to do, teenage mothers passing crack over baby diapers? And then she told us what happened one afternoon when she went to town to get groceries, and the local high school was having the homecoming parade for their football team, the Cowboys, with a band and horns and the whole town there to watch. They were playing the Indians from the high school in the next county, and so all the players on the team were dressed up like cowboys and riding in the beds of Fords, and behind each truck they dragged a plastic Indian in a noose. They went around town three times, she and her uncle waiting to be able to get through. Did we understand what that meant? Did it sound like good clean fun? Did it?

I suggested to Leticiana that *she* knew something about something—and that here was the root of an argument, the personal example that offered a stake in the discourse, that all she had to learn to do was write it. And while there was little "correct" or standard grammar in Leticiana's speech, and though working through the grammatical issues without eliminating her voice took time and effort, she had *style*. She had a voice that should and could be heard. She also had a long way to go to succeed at the University of Oregon— but when she saw, in conference after conference with me, that I cared and that I wanted her only to do her best, she invested. I came to look forward to the high-waving hand, the emphatic call of *Teach-er!* She earned a B, a B+, a grudging A-; her grammar improved as she read and worked in her other classes. By her last essay, on identity, she wrote me not one, but three different essays about the meaning of education and its role in her identity. Each essay was excellent and different: what a higher education means to a student coming from the sort of poverty she'd experienced with an absentee father, a mother caught in a cycle of poverty and afflicted by health issues, and her close family caught up in drugs and petty crime out of the desire for something better and brighter than what was before them. What sort of curriculum might reach a student like her, interested in so much and with so little to hold onto at a place like Oregon. And what the price was for achieving excellence in the face of adversity—the personal sacrifice, the weight of everyone else's expectations.

Each of the essays would have been worthy of an A. Taken together, I contemplated the possibility of the A+.

Over the summer, Leticiana and I emailed back and forth a couple of times—I'd written her a letter for a transfer to the University of Southern California, but she'd decided to stay in Oregon. She wrote me an email thanking me for the letter, starting out: "Dear Mr. Mike (I feel I should call you that now)." It was a nice letter telling me about how she was working two jobs that summer trying to help her mother make rent, how badly she missed school. Yet I took issue with "Mr. Mike"—why was "Mike" coming from Leticiana, whose calls of "Teacher!" had punctuated my entire year? I wrote that I missed "Teacher." She replied the next day:

> About calling you Mr. Mike: When I was in high school,
> most of the teachers and students didn't have a close
> bond with one another. Washington was huge, and
> it was real real poor, and the classes were forty and
> fifty students to a class. The teachers rarely knew the
> students by name, and all the students just called their
> teachers, "Teacher." You were the first instructor I had

here, and it was a force of habit to call you, "Teacher."
It seemed to have made me feel more comfortable with
you because you always found it so funny. But you
weren't like those teachers at Washington—you knew
my name. You believed in me. So it seems only fair that
I give you a name.

    Thanks, Mr. Mike.
    Leticiana.

America's schools are full of Leticianas, children who deserve a life better than they were born into. They walk the streets right now, some on the hot, dusty streets of the wrong side of the tracks in faraway places like the Delta, others out of sight in windowless apartments just off a suburban street, still more boxed into urban blocks: so many bright, good kids, some loud and flamboyant, some quiet and scared, kids walking with their heads down because they don't know what else to do.

They should be seen, be named, and have their voices heard. They deserve more than can be offered.

ACKNOWLEDGMENTS

To my family; I owe you everything, always, and love you all.

Thanks to my readers and friends in the literary world and beyond, without whom this book would not exist (in order unrelated to importance): Heather Ryan, J. T. Bushnell, Kirstin Valdez Quade, Ru Freeman, Chris Harvey, Adrienne Gunn, Nita Noveno, Tim Dalton, Michelle Penaloza, Ebony Haight, Marie Carvalho, Caroline Comerford, Elissa Wald, Molly Reid, Jay Nebel, Amanda LeBrun Anderson, Jenny Liou, Carmiel Banasky, Danielle Seid, Tarn MacArthur, Matthew Salesses, David Daniels, Joe Wilkins, Jessica Nelson, Stacie Michelle Williams, Mark Sleiter, Tim Horvath, Paul Martone, Carolyn Berquist, Miriam Gershow, Keetje Kuipers, Justin King, Caitlyn Hayes, Elyse Fenton, Kim Thompson, and the Oregon Writers Collective in general.

Thanks too to those whose judgment, mentorship, editorial aid, and encouragement helped inform this work, including David Bradley, Ehud Havazelet, Jason Brown, Travis Kurowski, Tom Williams, Amanda M. Fairbanks, Hattie Fletcher, Erin Stalcup, Bill and Chloe Hedden, Scott Russell Sanders, Katie Dykstra, and Ralph Eubanks. Special thanks to all who were with me in the Delta and supported me there, including all teachers and the strong leadership of my school (Principal B, all the Mrs. Bs), and most especially Kiersten, Aron, Edlyn, Michael, Rachel, Kara, Jenny, Bennett, Ellen, Laura, Mekia, and Meg. In their essential support, I thank Ron, Alex, Rachel, and Del.

Special thanks to Kent Wolf for seeing this book through and helping give it shape, and to the University Press of Mississippi for giving it a home. Parts of this memoir appeared in some form in *Creative Nonfiction*'s "Southern Sin" issue, *Creative Nonfiction*'s anthology *Becoming a Teacher*, *Guernica*, the *Oxford American*, *Gulf Coast*, *Salon*, *Waxwing*, *GOOD* online, *Southword*, *Bacon*, and the Good Men Project.